SUPER EASY SONGBOOK

Disney **HITS**

T0105915

ISBN 978-1-70518-323-6

HAL•LEONARD®

Visit Hal Leonard Online at
www.halleonard.com

World headquarters, contact:
Hal Leonard
7777 West Bluemound Road
Milwaukee, WI 53213
Email: info@halleonard.com

In Europe, contact:
Hal Leonard Europe Limited
1 Red Place
London, W1K 6PL
Email: info@halleonardeurope.com

In Australia, contact:
Hal Leonard Australia Pty. Ltd.
4 Lentara Court
Cheltenham, Victoria, 3192 Australia
Email: info@halleonard.com.au

Welcome to the *Super Easy Songbook* series!

This unique collection will help you play your favorite songs quickly and easily. Here's how it works:

- Play the simplified melody with your right hand. Letter names appear inside each note to assist you.

- There are no key signatures to worry about! If a sharp ♯ or flat ♭ is needed, it is shown beside the note each time.

- There are no page turns, so your hands never have to leave the keyboard.

- If two notes are connected by a tie ⌣, hold the first note for the combined number of beats. (The second note does not show a letter name since it is not re-struck.)

- Add basic chords with your left hand using the provided keyboard diagrams. Chord voicings have been carefully chosen to minimize hand movement.

- The left-hand rhythm is up to you, and chord notes can be played together or separately. Be creative!

- If the chords sound muddy, move your left hand an octave* higher. If this gets in the way of playing the melody, move your right hand an octave higher as well.

   * *An octave spans eight notes. If your starting note is C, the next C to the right is an octave higher.*

―――――――――――――――― ALSO AVAILABLE ――――――――――――――――

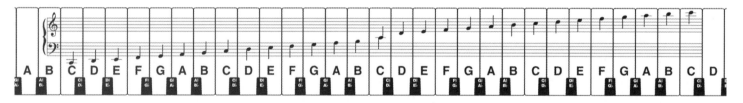

Hal Leonard Student Keyboard Guide HL00296039

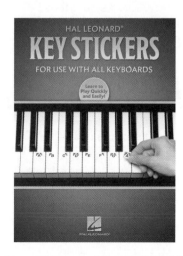

Key Stickers HL00100016

4	All I Want	50	Look Through My Eyes
6	All Is Found	52	Love Is an Open Door
8	Almost There	54	Loyal Brave True
10	The Ballad of the Lonesome Cowboy	56	Nobody Like U
12	Chillin' Like a Villain	58	Once Upon a Dream
14	Cruella De Vil	60	The Place Where Lost Things Go
16	Dos Oruguitas	62	Queen of Mean
18	Evermore	64	Reindeer(s) Are Better Than People
20	Ev'rybody Wants to Be a Cat	66	Remember Me (Ernesto de la Cruz)
22	For the First Time in Forever	68	The Rose Song
24	Happy Working Song	70	Seize the Day
26	Hawaiian Roller Coaster Ride	72	Show Yourself
28	He's a Pirate	74	So Close
9	Hot Dog!	76	Speechless
30	How Does a Moment Last Forever	78	Spirit
32	How Far I'll Go	80	Surface Pressure
34	I Just Can't Wait to Be King	82	Trust in Me (The Python's Song)
36	If I Didn't Have You	84	Un Poco Loco
38	If Only	86	We Don't Talk About Bruno
40	In Summer	88	When Will My Life Begin?
42	Into the Unknown	90	You Can't Stop the Girl
44	Lead the Way	92	You'll Be in My Heart (Pop Version)
46	Les Poissons	94	You're Welcome
48	Let's Get Together		

All I Want
from HIGH SCHOOL MUSICAL: THE MUSICAL: THE SERIES

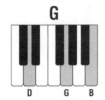 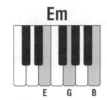 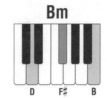 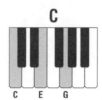 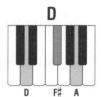

Music and Lyrics by
Olivia Rodrigo

Moderately slow

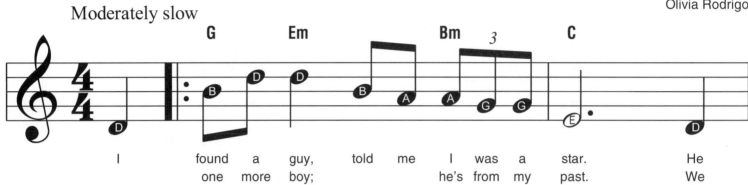

I found a guy, told me I was a star. He
one more boy; he's from my past. We

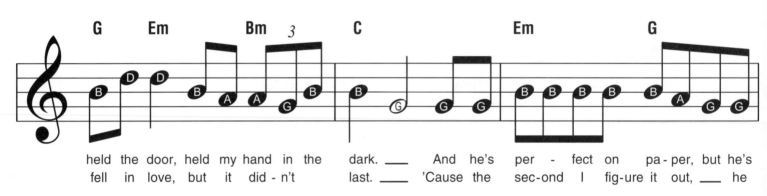

held the door, held my hand in the dark. ___ And he's per-fect on pa-per, but he's
fell in love, but it did-n't last. ___ 'Cause the sec-ond I fig-ure it out, ___ he

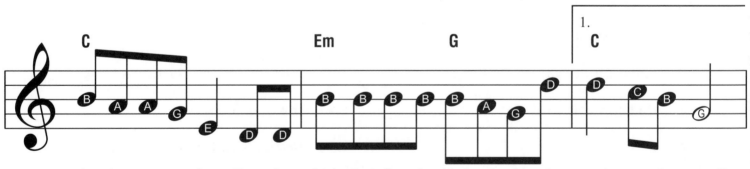

ly-ing to my face. Does he think that I'm the kind of girl who needs to be saved?
push-es me a-way. And I won't ___ fight for love if you won't

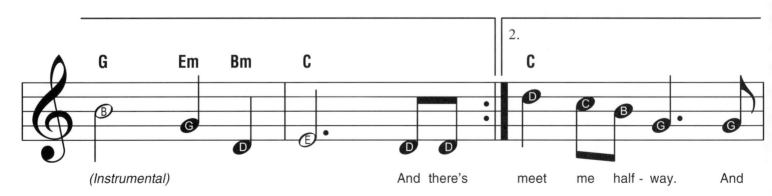

(Instrumental)
And there's meet me half-way. And

All Is Found
from FROZEN 2

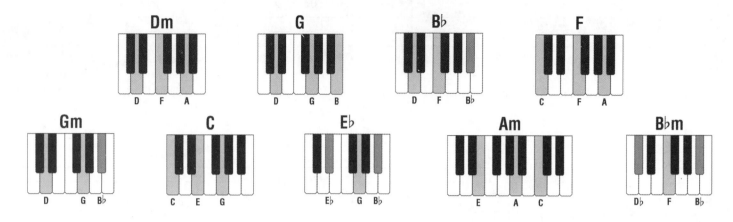

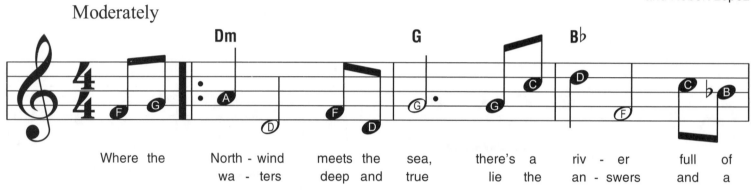

Music and Lyrics by Kristen Anderson-Lopez
and Robert Lopez

Moderately

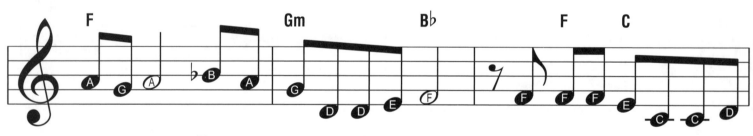

Where the North - wind meets the sea, there's a riv - er full of
wa - ters deep and true lie the an - swers and a

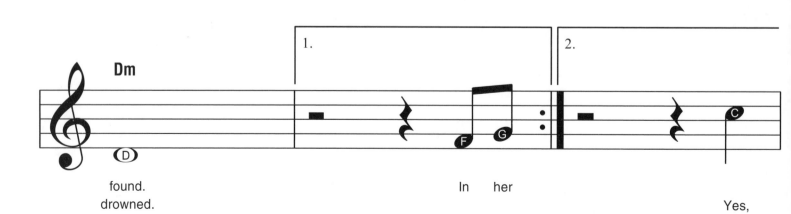

mem - o - ry. Sleep, my dar - ling, safe and sound, for in this riv - er, all is
path for you. Dive down deep in - to her sound, but not too far, or you'll be

found.   In her
drowned.   Yes,

7

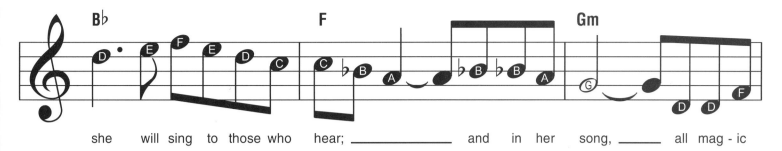

she will sing to those who hear; _____ and in her song, _____ all mag - ic

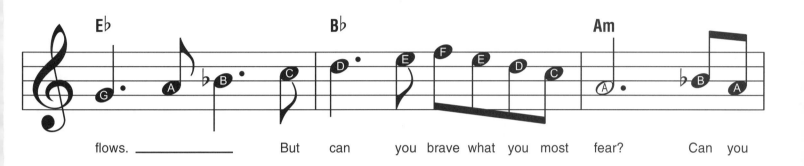

flows. _____ But can you brave what you most fear? Can you

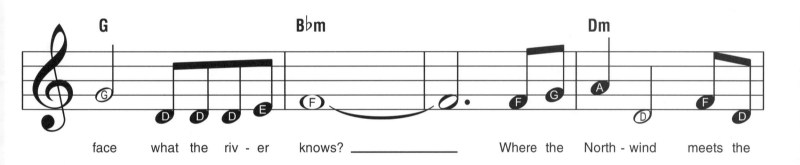

face what the riv - er knows? _____ Where the North - wind meets the

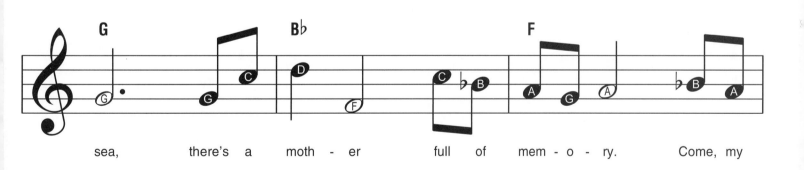

sea, there's a moth - er full of mem - o - ry. Come, my

dar - ling, home - ward bound. When all is lost, then all is found.

Almost There
from THE PRINCESS AND THE FROG

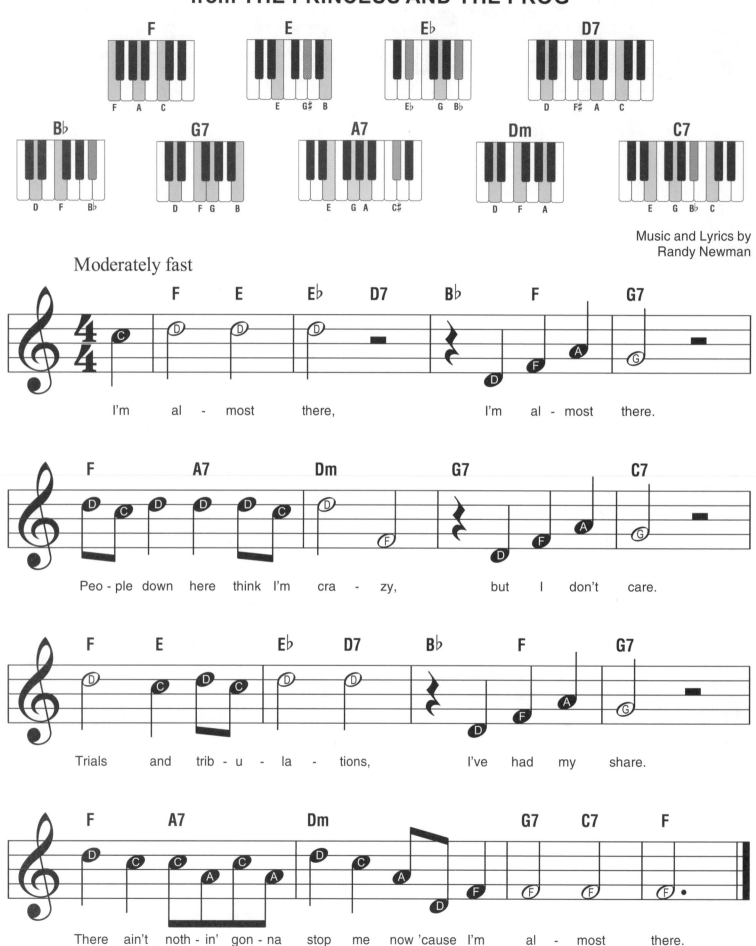

Music and Lyrics by
Randy Newman

Hot Dog!

from MICKEY MOUSE CLUB HOUSE

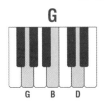
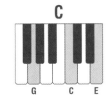
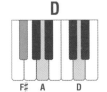
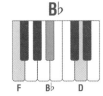

Words and Music by John Flansburgh
and John Linnell

Brightly, with a half-time feel

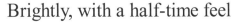

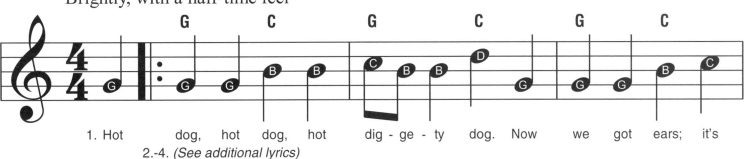

1. Hot dog, hot dog, hot dig-ge-ty dog. Now we got ears; it's

2.-4. *(See additional lyrics)*

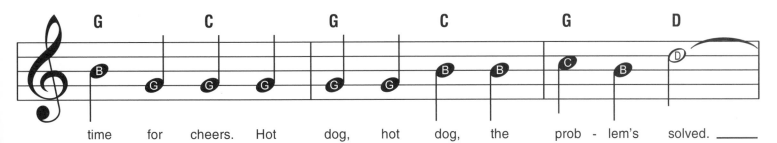

time for cheers. Hot dog, hot dog, the prob-lem's solved. _____

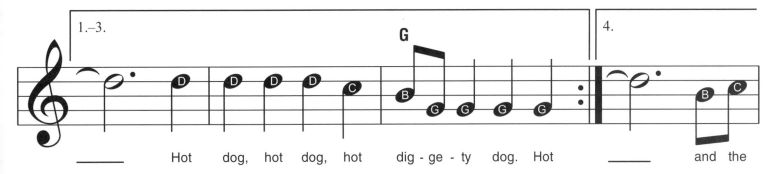

_____ Hot dog, hot dog, hot dig-ge-ty dog. Hot _____ and the

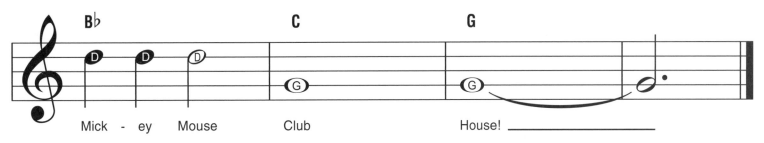

Mick-ey Mouse Club House! _____

Additional Lyrics

2. Hot dog, hot dog, hot diggety dog.
We're takin' off, we're dancin' now.
Hot dog, leap frog and holy cow!
Hot dog, hot dog, hot diggety dog.

3. Hot dog, hot dog, hot diggety dog.
It's a brand-new day; whatcha waitin' for?
Get up, stretch out, stomp on the floor.
Hot dog, hot dog, hot diggety dog.

4. Hot dog, hot dog, hot diggety dog.
We're splittin' the scene, we're full of beans.
So long for now from Mickey Mouse
And the Mickey Mouse Club House!

The Ballad of the Lonesome Cowboy
from TOY STORY 4

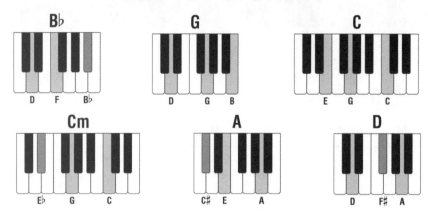

Music and Lyrics by
Randy Newman

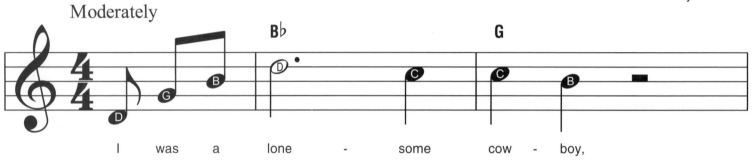

I was a lone - some cow - boy,

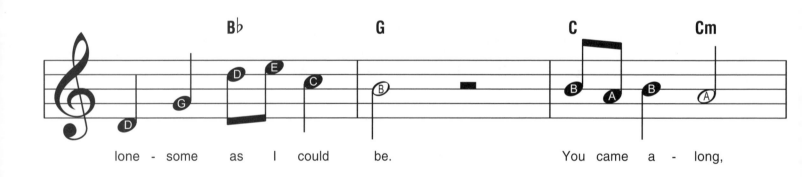

lone - some as I could be. You came a - long,

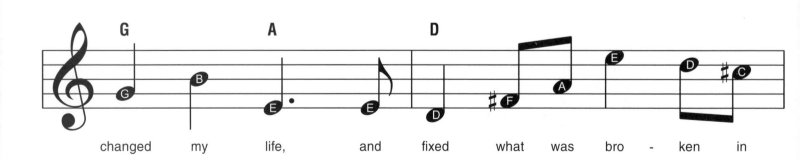

changed my life, and fixed what was bro - ken in

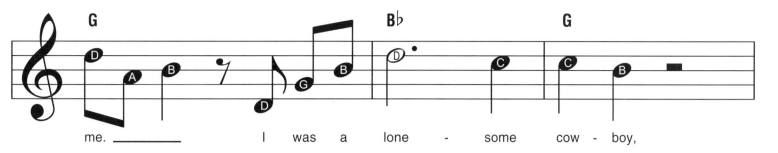

me. _____ I was a lone - some cow - boy,

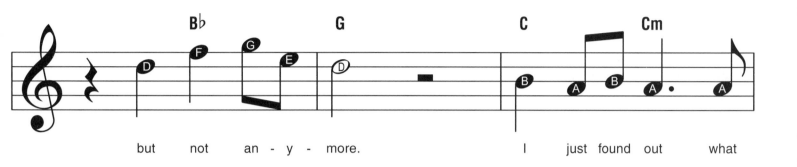

but not an - y - more. I just found out what

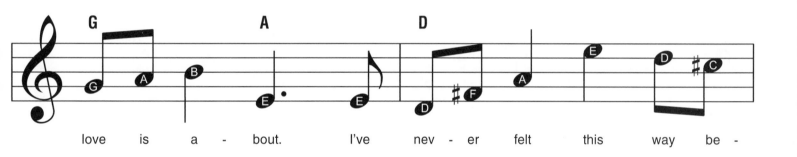

love is a - bout. I've nev - er felt this way be -

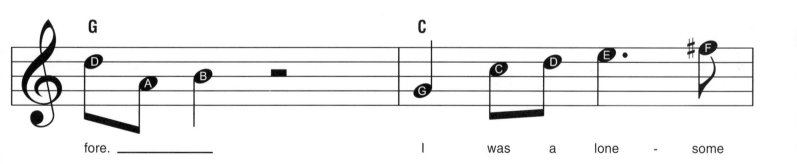

fore. _____ I was a lone - some

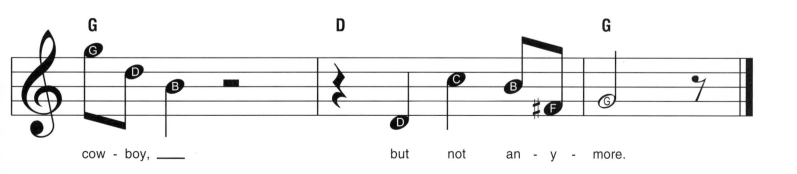

cow - boy, ___ but not an - y - more.

Chillin' Like a Villain
from DESCENDANTS 2

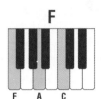
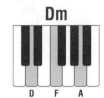
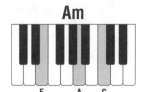
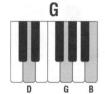

Written by Antonina Armato,
Tim James, Thomas Sturges
and Adam Schmalholz

Moderate Dance groove

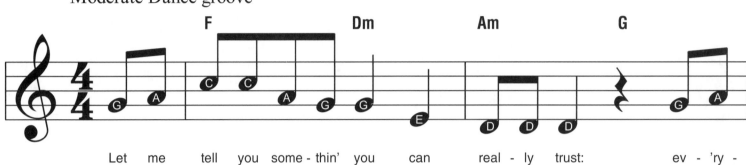

Let me tell you some-thin' you can real-ly trust: ev-'ry-

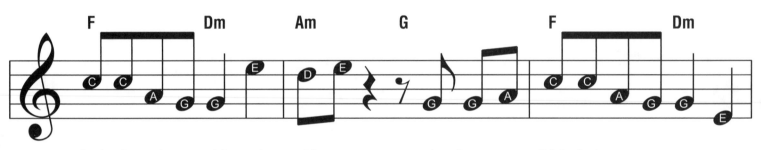

bod-y's got a wick-ed side. ___ I know you think that you can nev-er

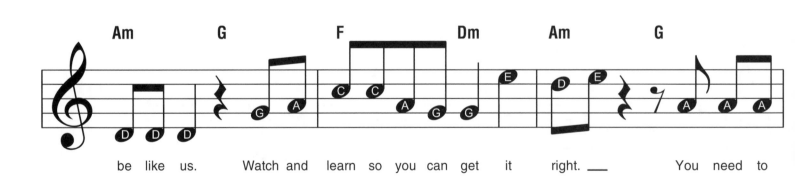

be like us. Watch and learn so you can get it right. ___ You need to

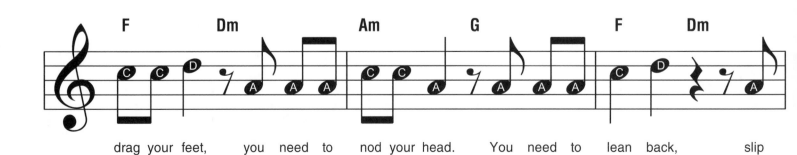

drag your feet, you need to nod your head. You need to lean back, slip

Cruella De Vil
from 101 DALMATIANS

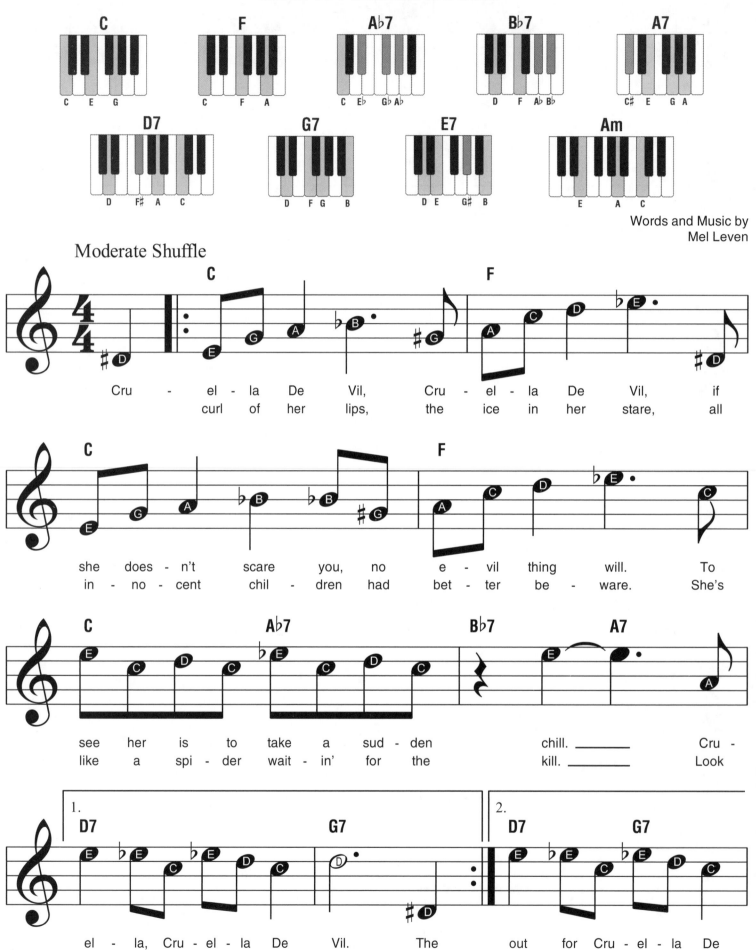

Words and Music by
Mel Leven

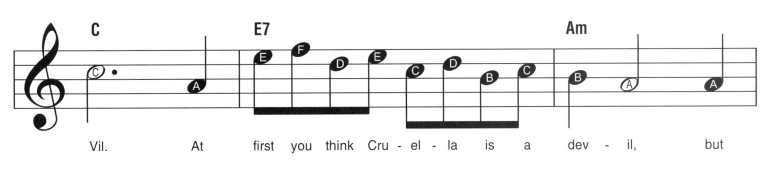

Vil. At first you think Cru-el-la is a dev-il, but

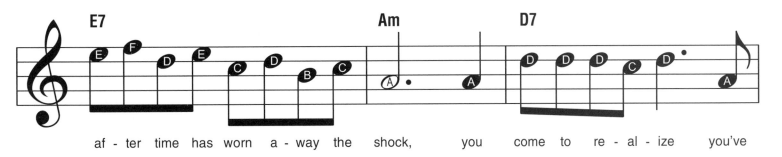

af-ter time has worn a-way the shock, you come to re-al-ize you've

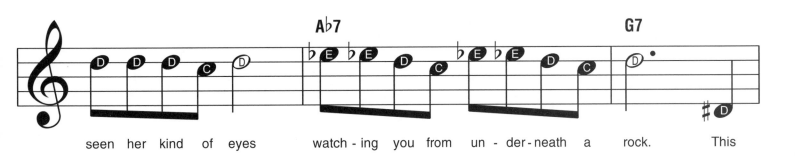

seen her kind of eyes watch-ing you from un-der-neath a rock. This

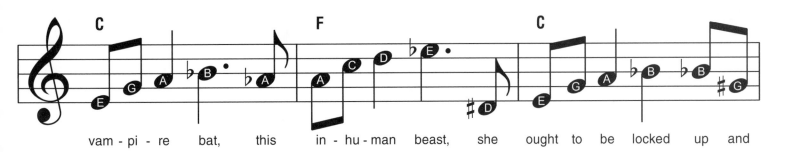

vam-pi-re bat, this in-hu-man beast, she ought to be locked up and

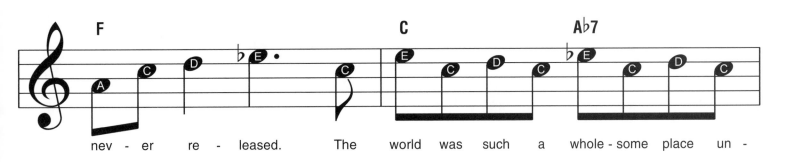

nev-er re-leased. The world was such a whole-some place un-

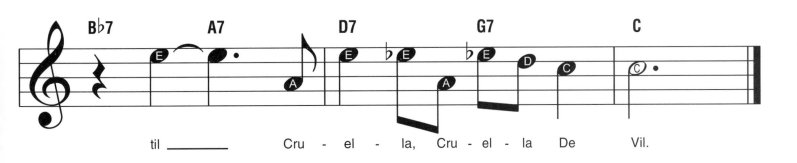

til _____ Cru-el-la, Cru-el-la De Vil.

Dos Oruguitas
from ENCANTO

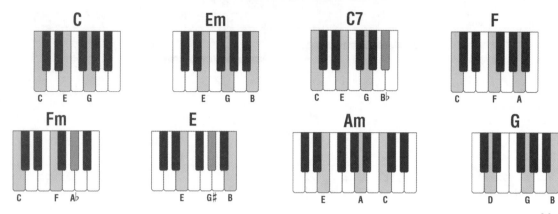

Music and Lyrics by
Lin-Manuel Miranda

Syncopated groove

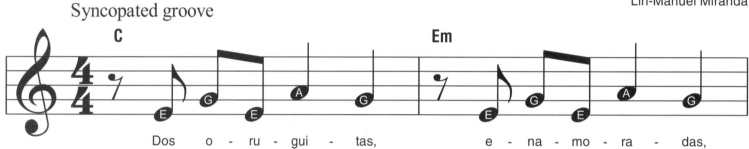

Dos o - ru - gui - tas,   e - na - mo - ra - das,
Dos o - ru - gui - tas   pa - ran el vien - to,

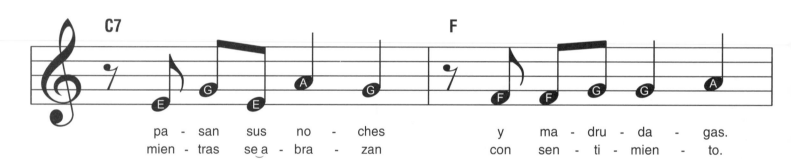

pa - san sus no - ches   y ma - dru - da - gas.
mien - tras se a - bra - zan   con sen - ti - mien - to.

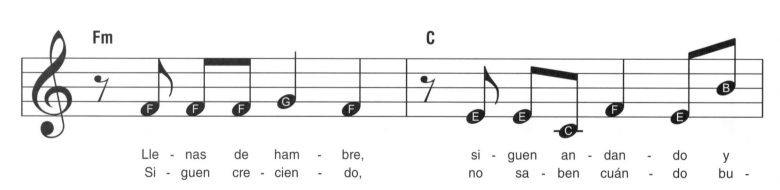

Lle - nas de ham - bre,   si - guen an - dan - do y
Si - guen cre - cien - do,   no sa - ben cuán - do bu -

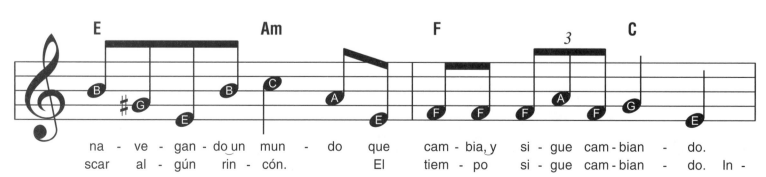

na - ve - gan - do un mun - do que cam - bia, y si - gue cam - bian - do.
scar al - gún rin - cón.   El tiem - po si - gue cam - bian - do. In -

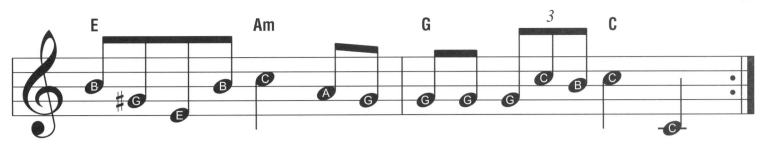

Na - ve - gan - do un mun - do que cam - bia, y si - gue cam - bian - do.
se - pa - ra - bles son, y el tiem - po si - gue cam - bian - do.

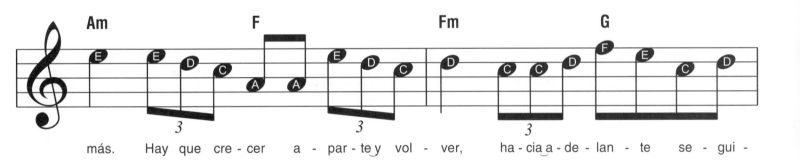

Ay, or - u - gui - tas, no se a - guan - ten

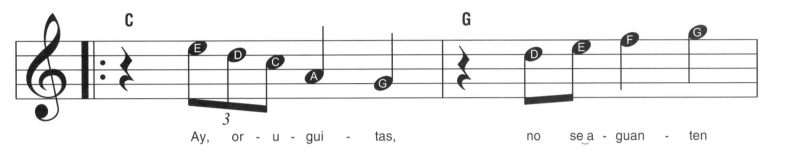

más. Hay que cre - cer a - par - te y vol - ver, ha - cia a - de - lan - te se - gui -

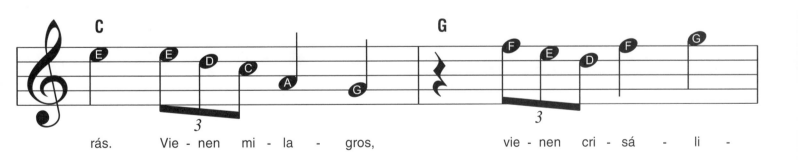

rás. Vie - nen mi - la - gros, vie - nen cri - sá - li -

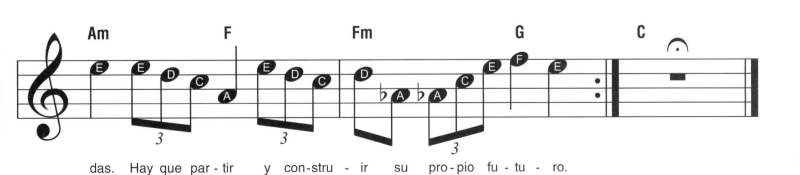

das. Hay que par - tir y con - stru - ir su pro - pio fu - tu - ro.

Evermore
from BEAUTY AND THE BEAST

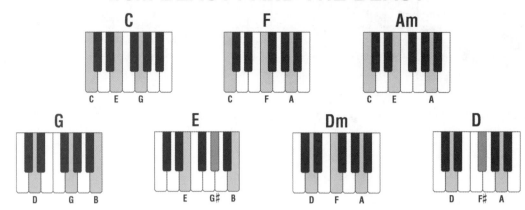

Music by Alan Menken
Lyrics by Tim Rice

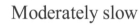

Moderately slow

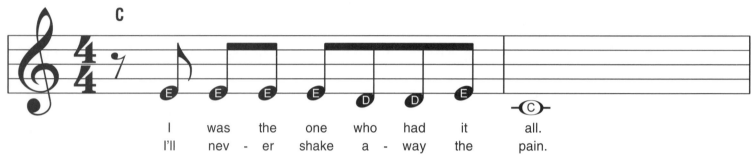

I was the one who had it all.
I'll nev - er shake a - way the pain.

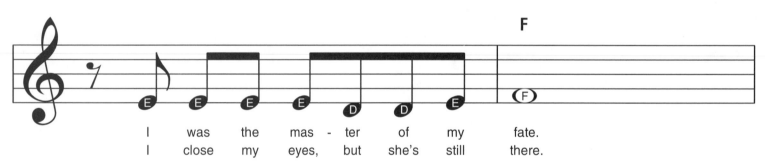

I was the mas - ter of my fate.
I close my eyes, but she's still there.

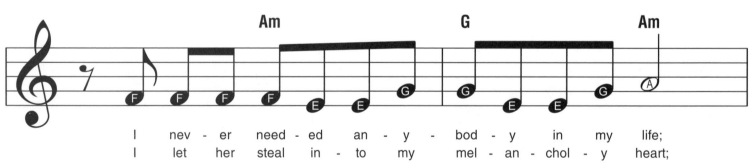

I nev - er need - ed an - y - bod - y in my life;
I let her steal in - to my mel - an - chol - y heart;

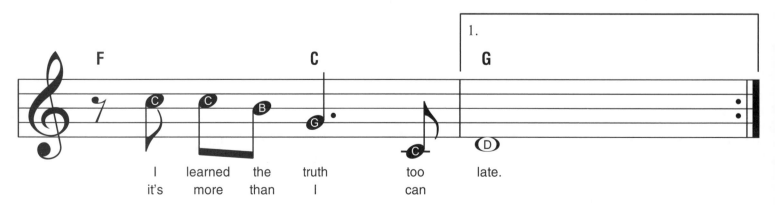

I learned the truth too late.
it's more than I can

Ev'rybody Wants to Be a Cat

from THE ARISTOCATS

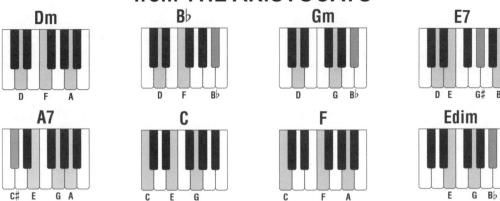

Words by Floyd Huddleston
Music by Al Rinker

Easy Shuffle

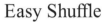

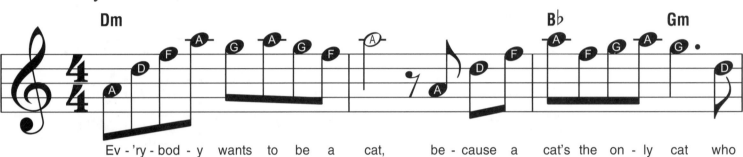

Ev - 'ry - bod - y wants to be a cat, be - cause a cat's the on - ly cat who

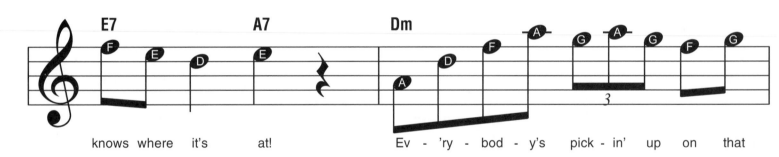

knows where it's at! Ev - 'ry - bod - y's pick - in' up on that

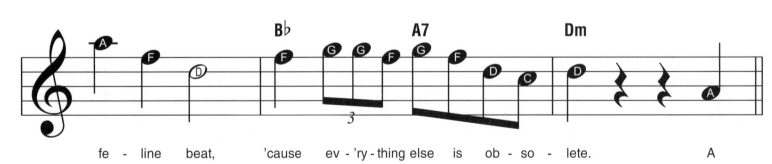

fe - line beat, 'cause ev - 'ry - thing else is ob - so - lete. A

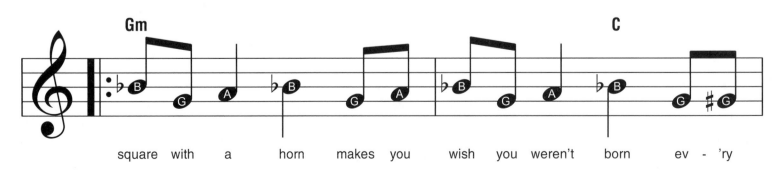

square with a horn makes you wish you weren't born ev - 'ry

For the First Time in Forever
from FROZEN

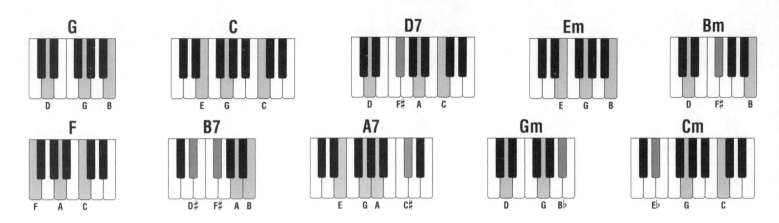

Music and Lyrics by Kristen Anderson-Lopez
and Robert Lopez

Moderately

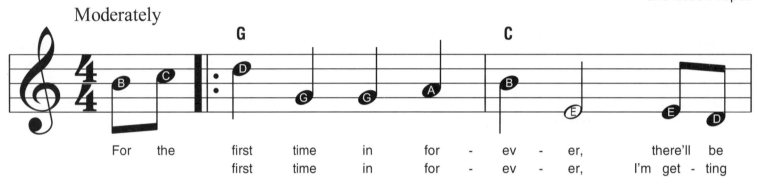

For the first time in for - ev - er, there'll be
first time in for - ev - er, I'm get - ting

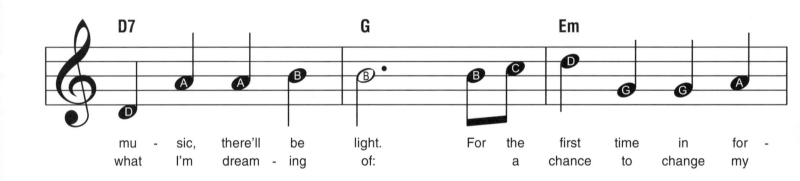

mu - sic, there'll be light. For the first time in for -
what I'm dream - ing of: a chance to change my

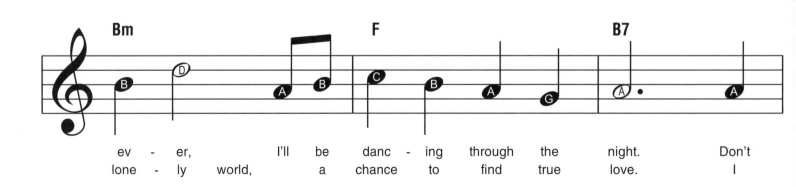

ev - er, I'll be danc - ing through the night. Don't
lone - ly world, a chance to find true love. I

know if I'm e-lat-ed or gas-sy, but I'm some-where in that zone. _____
know it all ends to-mor-row, so it has to be to-day. _____

1.
_____ 'Cause for the first time in for-ev-er,
_____ 'Cause for the

I won't be a-lone. For the

2.
first time in for-ev-er, for the first time in for-

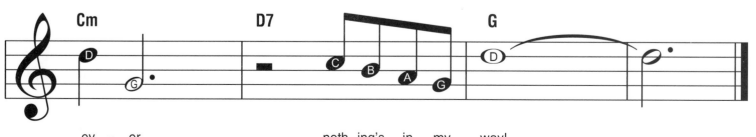

ev-er, noth-ing's in my way! _____

Happy Working Song
from ENCHANTED

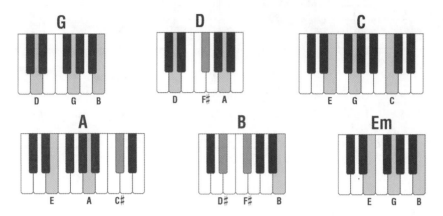

Music by Alan Menken
Lyrics by Stephen Schwartz

Perky and light

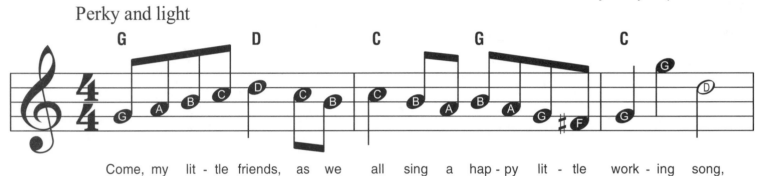

Come, my lit - tle friends, as we all sing a hap - py lit - tle work - ing song,

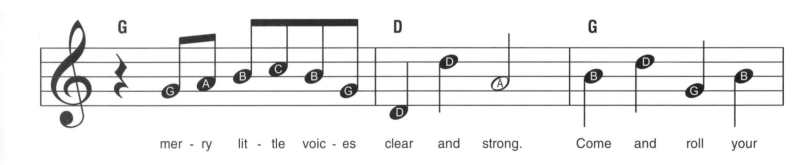

mer - ry lit - tle voic - es clear and strong. Come and roll your

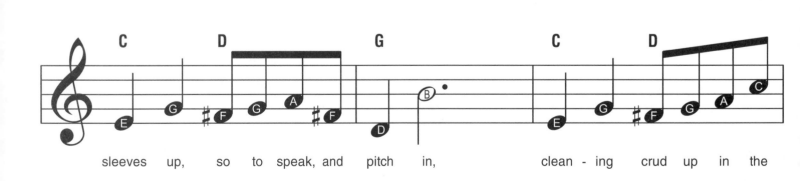

sleeves up, so to speak, and pitch in, clean - ing crud up in the

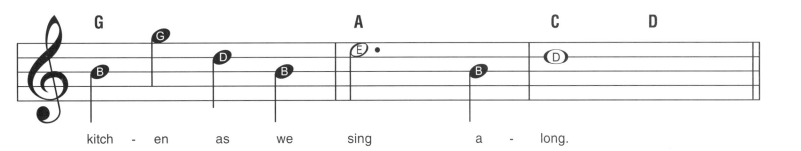

kitch - en as we sing a - long.

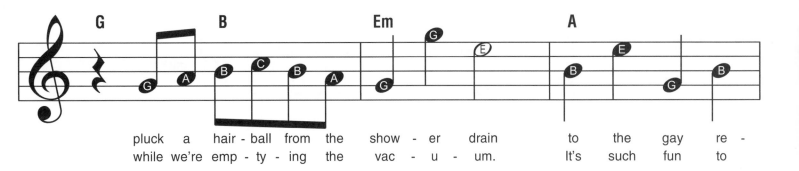

Trill a cheer - y tune in the tub as you scrub a stub - born mil - dew stain;
How we all en - joy let - ting loose with a lit - tle "la da dum dum dum"

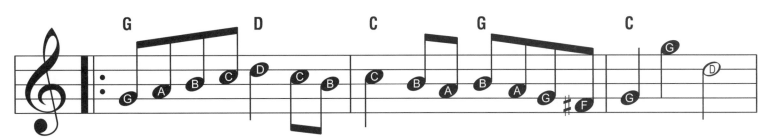

pluck a hair - ball from the show - er drain to the gay re -
while we're emp - ty - ing the vac - u - um. It's such fun to

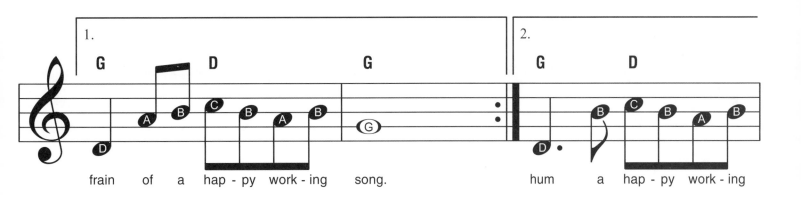

frain of a hap - py work - ing song.
hum a hap - py work - ing

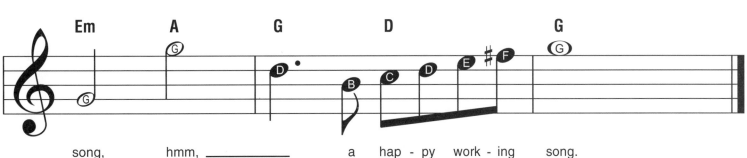

song, hmm, _____ a hap - py work - ing song.

Hawaiian Roller Coaster Ride

from LILO & STITCH

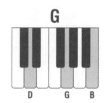 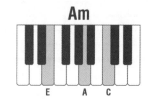 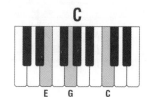 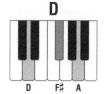

Words and Music by Alan Silvestri
and Mark Keali'i Ho'omalu

Moderately fast

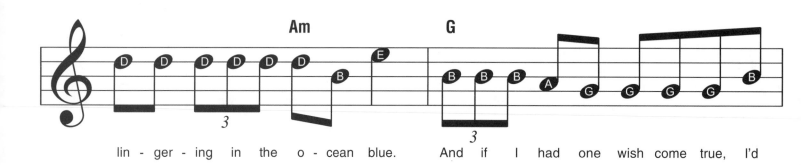

There's no place I'd rath-er be than on my surf-board out at sea,

lin-ger-ing in the o-cean blue. And if I had one wish come true, I'd

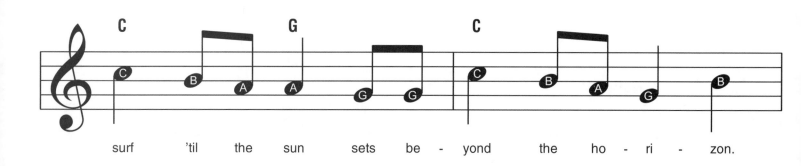

surf 'til the sun sets be-yond the ho-ri-zon.

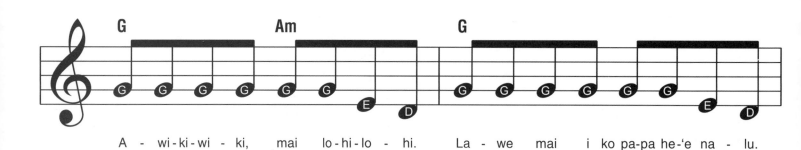

A - wi-ki-wi-ki, mai lo-hi-lo-hi. La-we mai i ko pa-pa he-'e na-lu.

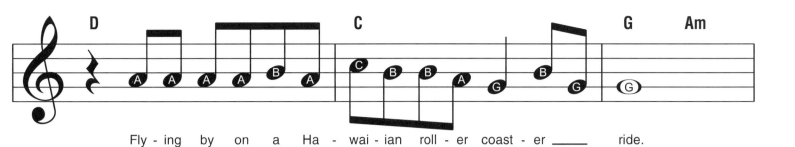

Fly - ing by on a Ha - wai - ian roll - er coast - er _____ ride.

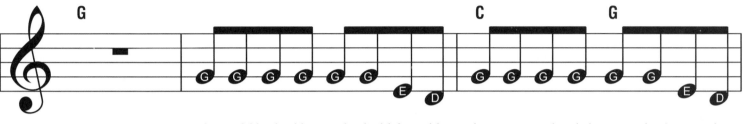

A - wi-ki-wi - ki, mai lo-hi-lo - hi. La - we mai i ko pa-pa he-'e na - lu.

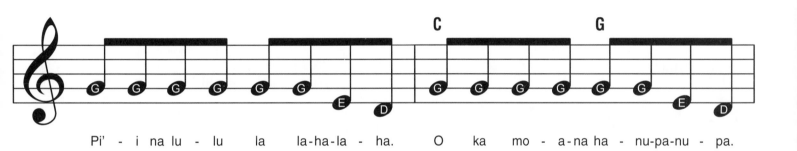

Pi' - i na lu - lu la la-ha-la - ha. O ka mo - a-na ha - nu-pa-nu - pa.

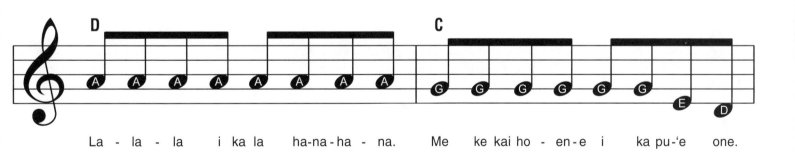

La - la - la i ka la ha-na-ha - na. Me ke kai ho - en-e i ka pu-'e one.

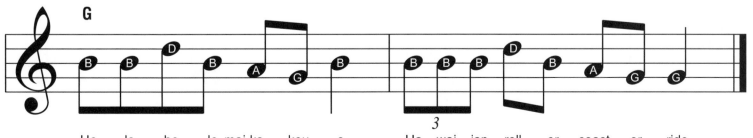

He - le - he - le mai ka kou e. Ha - wai - ian roll - er coast - er ride.

He's a Pirate
from PIRATES OF THE CARIBBEAN: THE CURSE OF THE BLACK PEARL

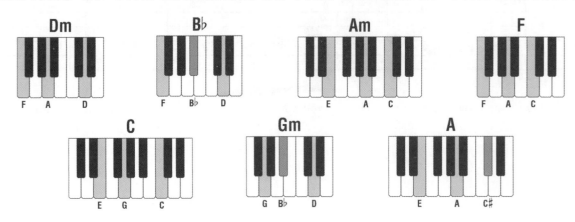

Written by Hans Zimmer,
Klaus Badelt and Geoff Zanelli

Briskly

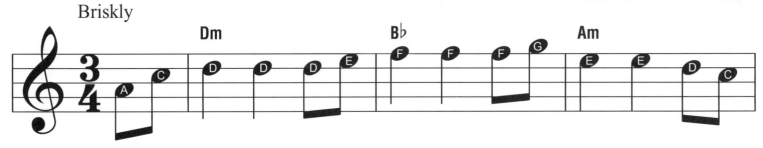

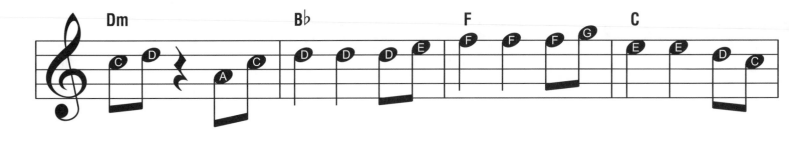

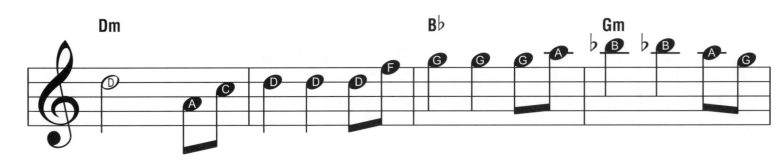

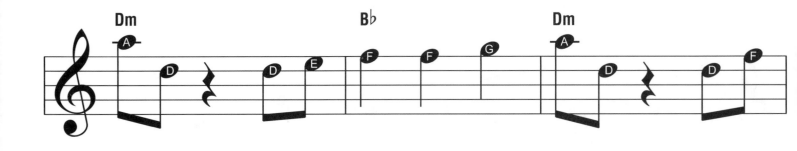

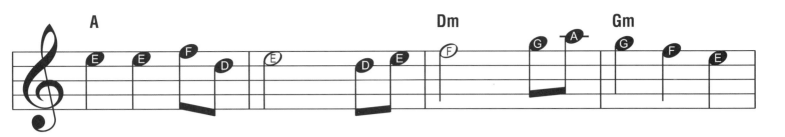

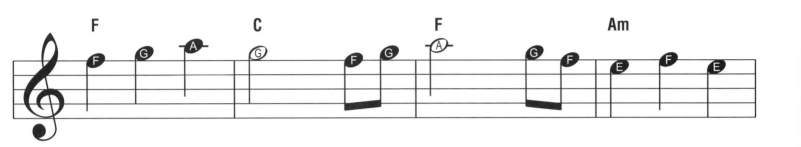

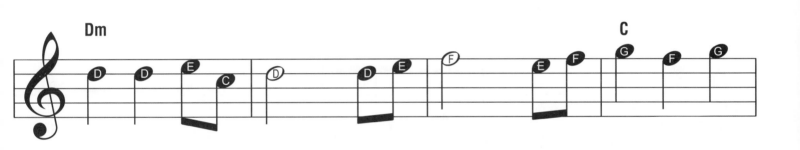

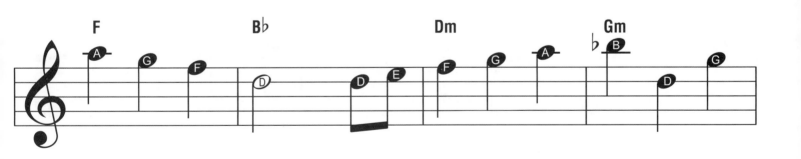

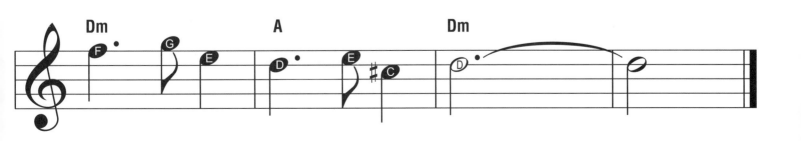

How Does a Moment Last Forever
from BEAUTY AND THE BEAST

Music by Alan Menken
Lyrics by Tim Rice

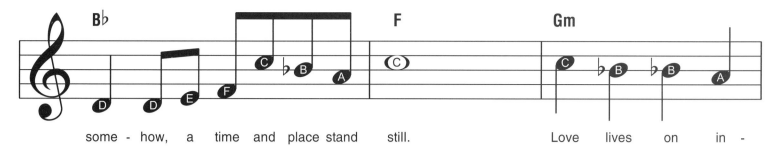

some - how, a time and place stand still. Love lives on in -

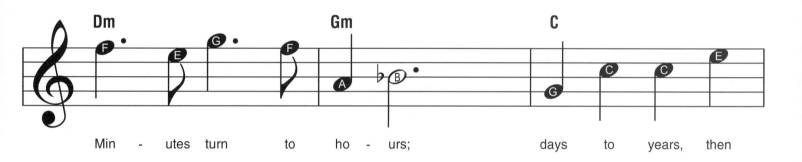

side our hearts, and al - ways will.

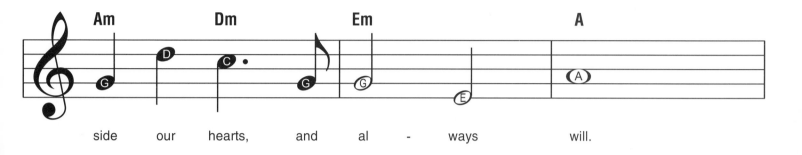

Min - utes turn to ho - urs; days to years, then

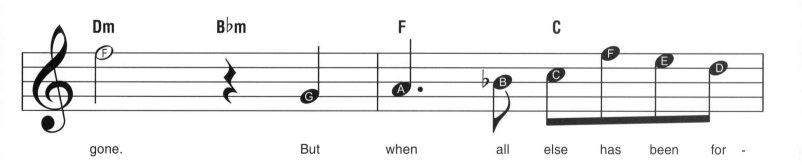

gone. But when all else has been for -

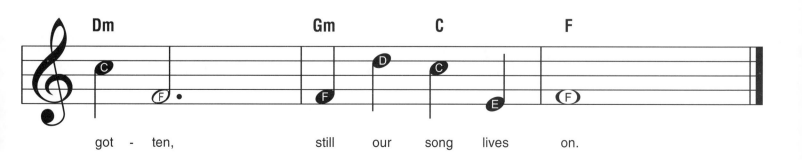

got - ten, still our song lives on.

How Far I'll Go
from MOANA

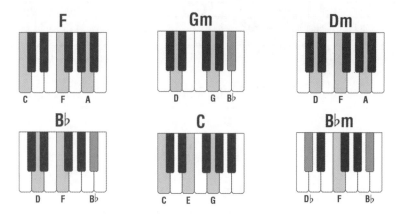

Music and Lyrics by
Lin-Manuel Miranda

Moderate half-time feel

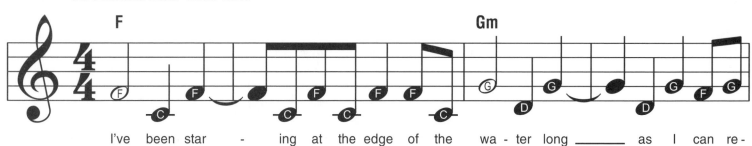

I've been star - ing at the edge of the wa - ter long _____ as I can re-

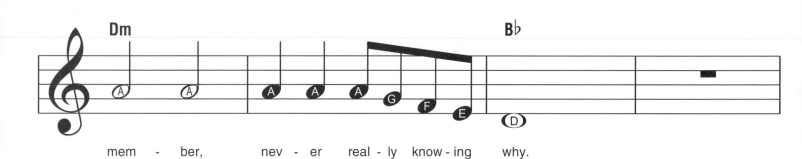

mem - ber, nev - er real - ly know - ing why.

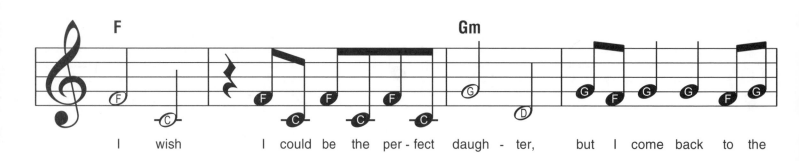

I wish I could be the per - fect daugh - ter, but I come back to the

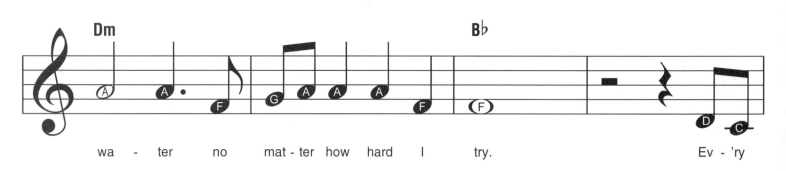

wa - ter no mat - ter how hard I try. Ev - 'ry

I Just Can't Wait to Be King

from THE LION KING

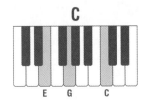
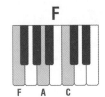
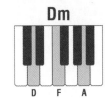
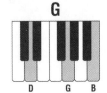

Music by Elton John
Lyrics by Tim Rice

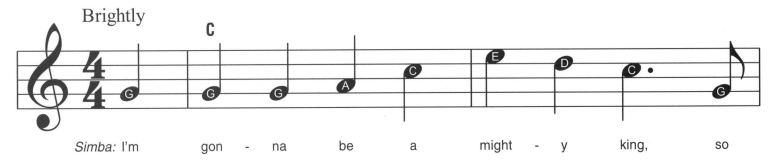

Simba: I'm gon - na be a might - y king, so

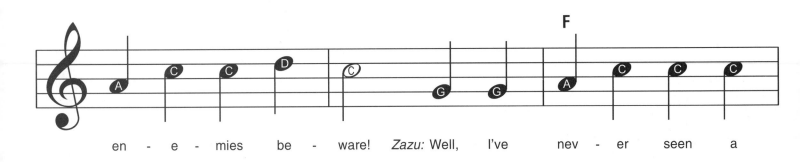

en - e - mies be - ware! Zazu: Well, I've nev - er seen a

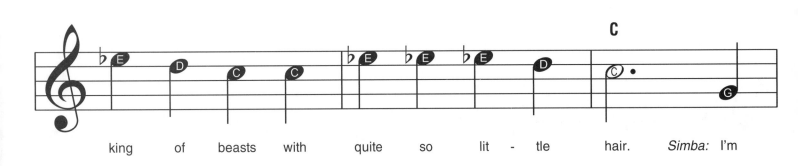

king of beasts with quite so lit - tle hair. Simba: I'm

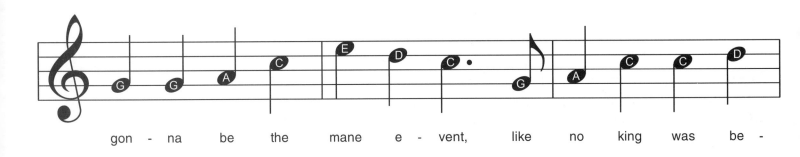

gon - na be the mane e - vent, like no king was be -

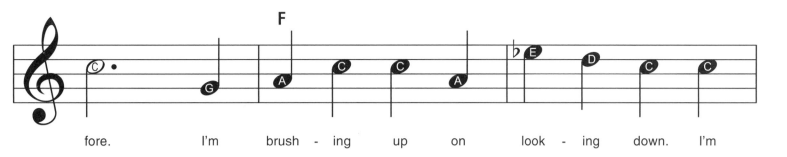

fore. I'm brush - ing up on look - ing down. I'm

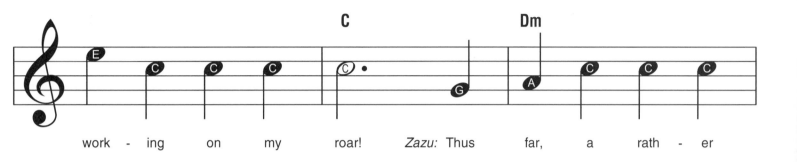

work - ing on my roar! *Zazu:* Thus far, a rath - er

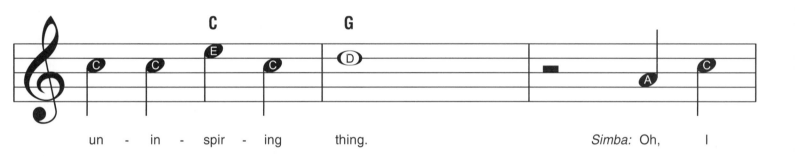

un - in - spir - ing thing. *Simba:* Oh, I

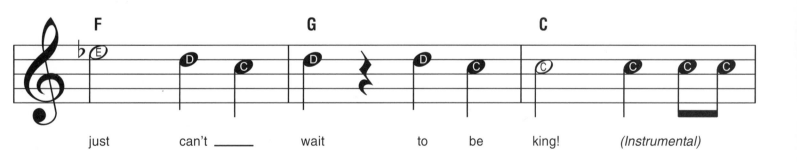

just can't _____ wait to be king! *(Instrumental)*

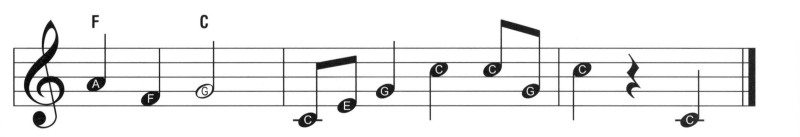

If I Didn't Have You

from MONSTERS, INC.

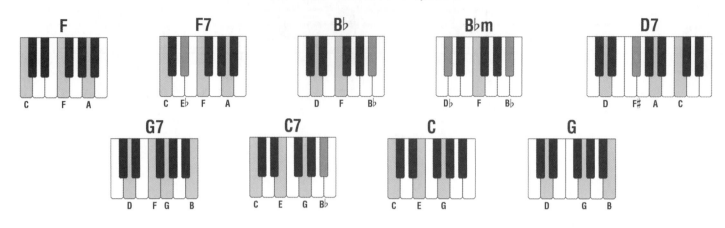

Music and Lyrics by
Randy Newman

Moderate Shuffle

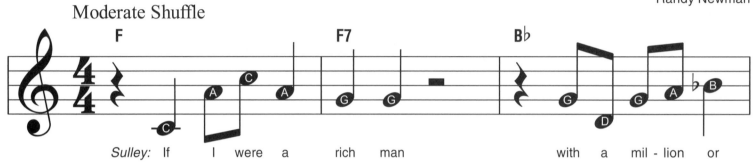

Sulley: If I were a rich man with a mil-lion or

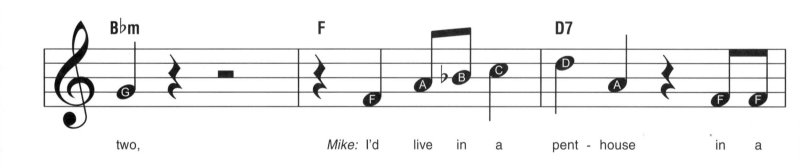

two, Mike: I'd live in a pent-house in a

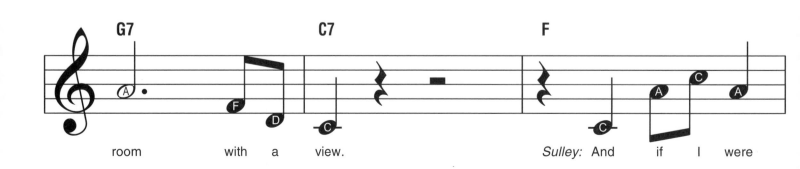

room with a view. Sulley: And if I were

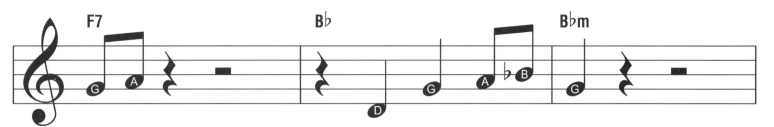

hand-some, (It could happen,) Sulley: 'cause dreams do come true,
Mike: (Spoken:) No way!

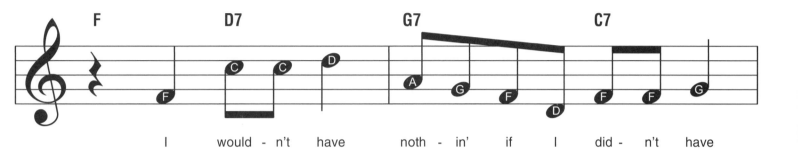

I would - n't have noth - in' if I did - n't have

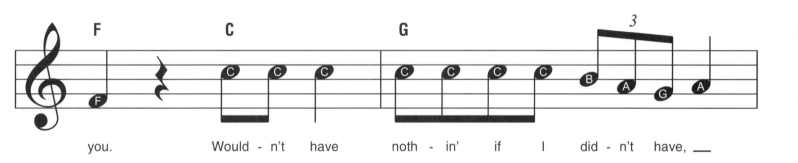

you. Would - n't have noth - in' if I did - n't have, ___

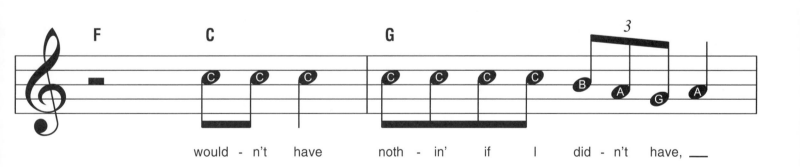

would - n't have noth - in' if I did - n't have, ___

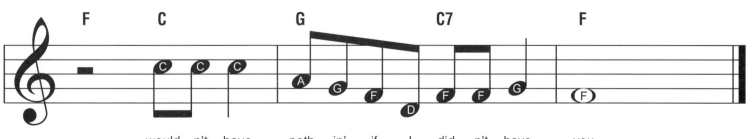

would - n't have noth - in' if I did - n't have you.

If Only
from DESCENDANTS

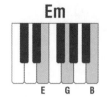
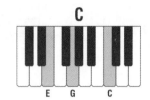

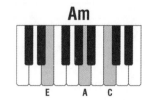
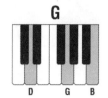

Words and Music by Adam Anders,
Nikki Hassman and Par Astrom

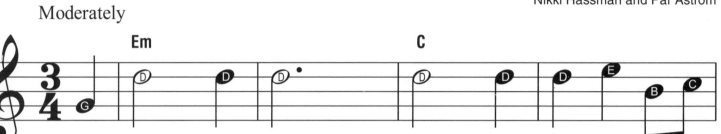

A mil - lion thoughts in my head. ___ Should I

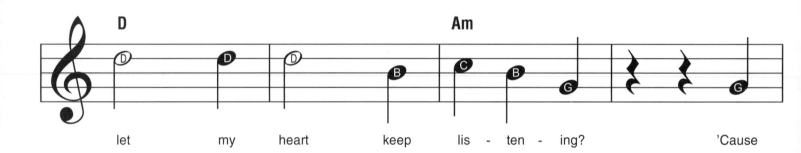

let my heart keep lis - ten - ing? 'Cause

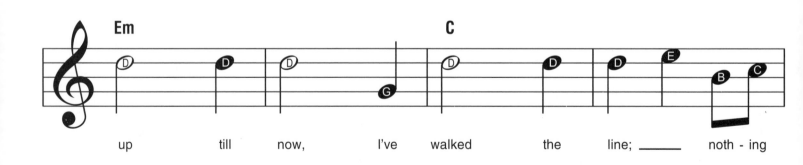

up till now, I've walked the line; ___ noth - ing

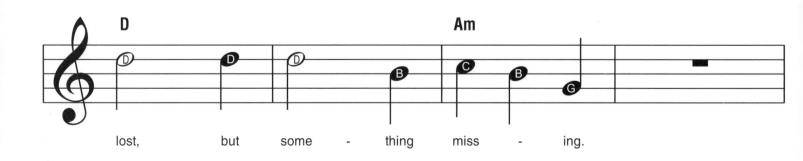

lost, but some - thing miss - ing.

In Summer
from FROZEN

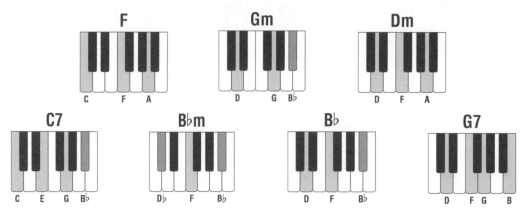

Music and Lyrics by Kristen Anderson-Lopez
and Robert Lopez

Happy Shuffle

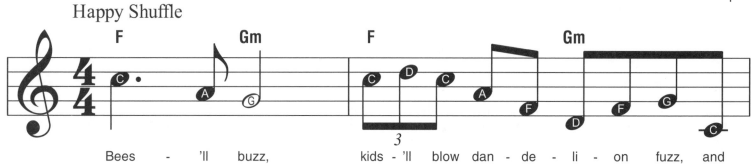

Bees - 'll buzz, kids - 'll blow dan - de - li - on fuzz, and

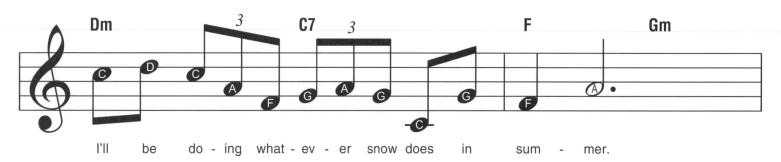

I'll be do - ing what - ev - er snow does in sum - mer.

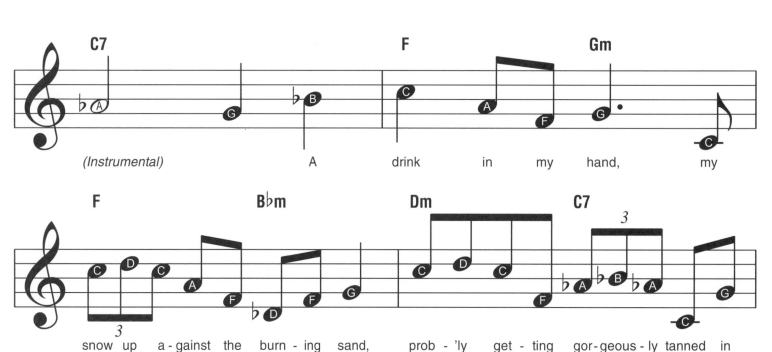

(Instrumental) A drink in my hand, my

snow up a - gainst the burn - ing sand, prob - 'ly get - ting gor - geous - ly tanned in

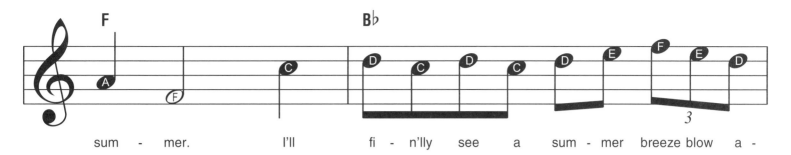

sum - mer. I'll fi - n'lly see a sum - mer breeze blow a -

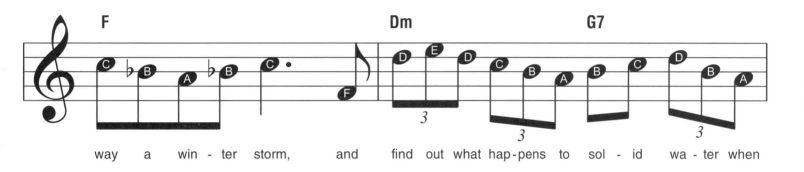

way a win - ter storm, and find out what hap - pens to sol - id wa - ter when

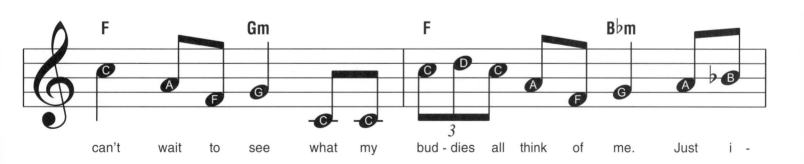

it gets warm. *(Instrumental)* And I

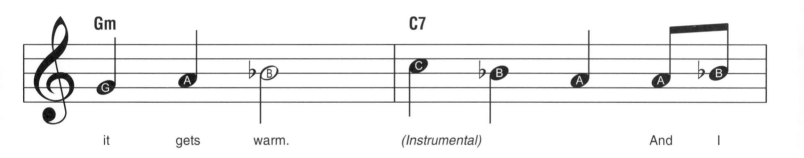

can't wait to see what my bud - dies all think of me. Just i -

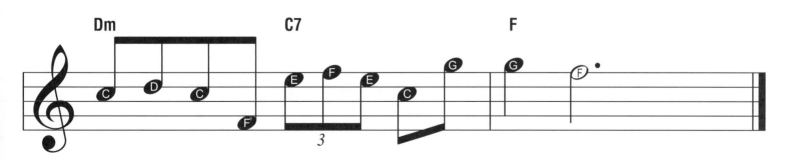

mag - ine how much cool - er I'll be in sum - mer!

Into the Unknown
from FROZEN 2

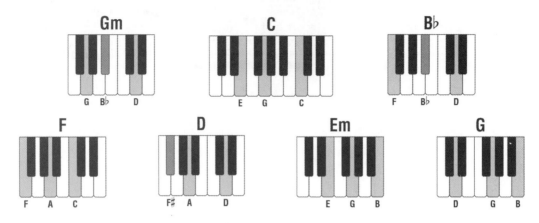

Music and Lyrics by Kristen Anderson-Lopez
and Robert Lopez

With determination

You're not a voice; you're just a ring-ing in my

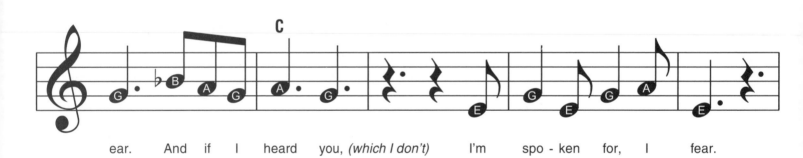

ear. And if I heard you, *(which I don't)* I'm spo-ken for, I fear.

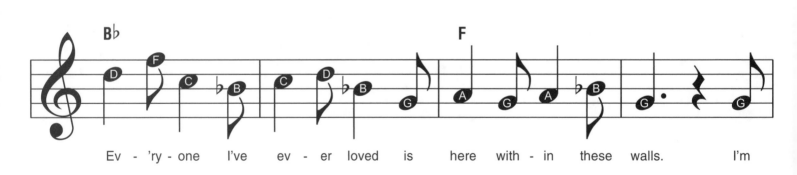

Ev-'ry-one I've ev-er loved is here with-in these walls. I'm

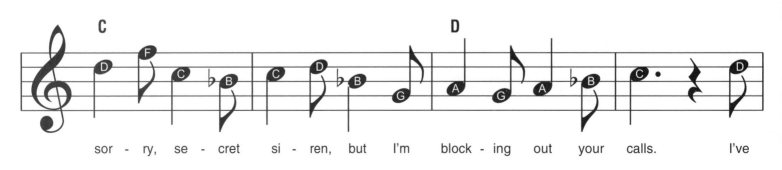

sor-ry, se-cret si-ren, but I'm block-ing out your calls. I've

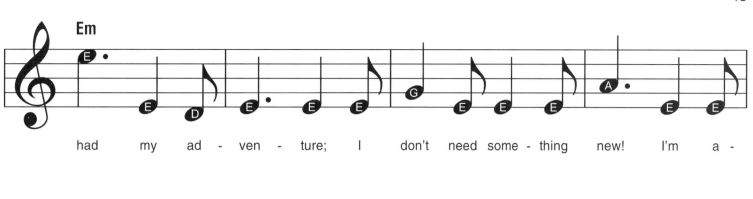

had my ad - ven - ture; I don't need some - thing new! I'm a -

fraid of what I'm risk - ing if I fol - low you in - to the un -

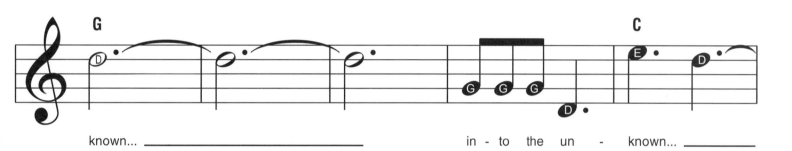

known... _____ in - to the un - known... _____

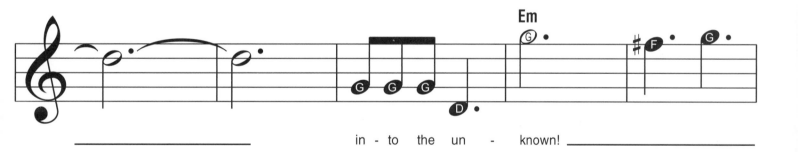

_____ in - to the un - known! _____

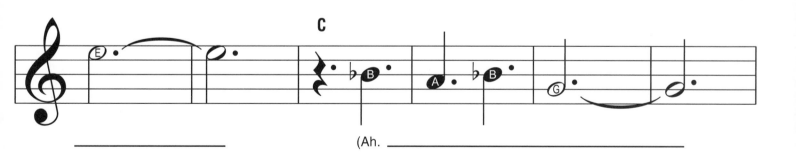

_____ (Ah. _____

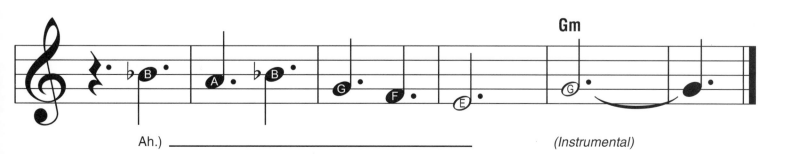

Ah.) _____ (Instrumental)

Lead the Way
from RAYA AND THE LAST DRAGON

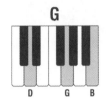
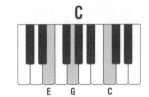
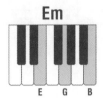

Music and Lyrics by
Jhené Aiko

Moderately

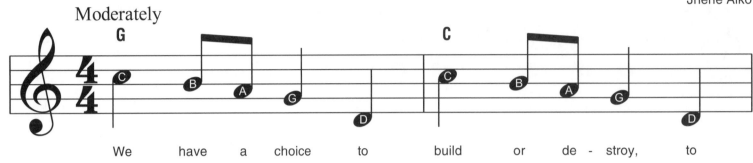

We have a choice to build or de - stroy, to

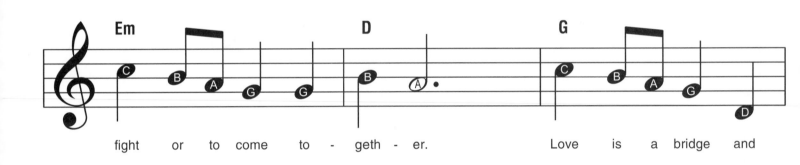

fight or to come to - geth - er. Love is a bridge and

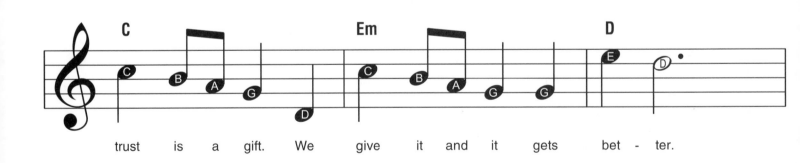

trust is a gift. We give it and it gets bet - ter.

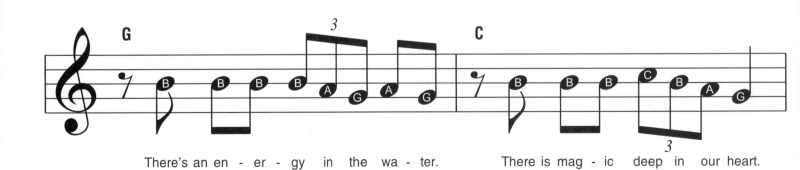

There's an en - er - gy in the wa - ter. There is mag - ic deep in our heart.

45

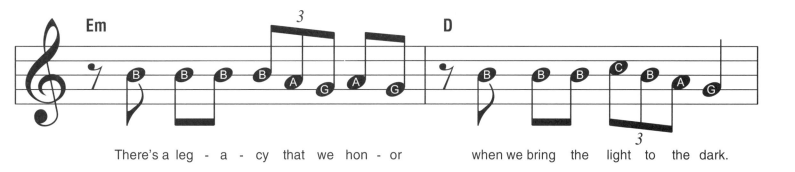

There's a leg - a - cy that we hon - or   when we bring the light to the dark.

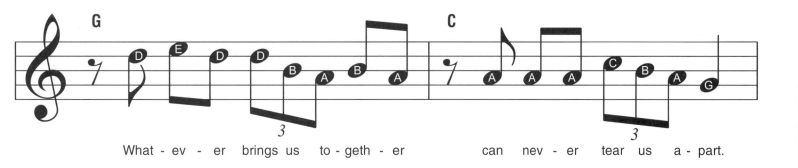

What - ev - er brings us to - geth - er   can nev - er tear us a - part.

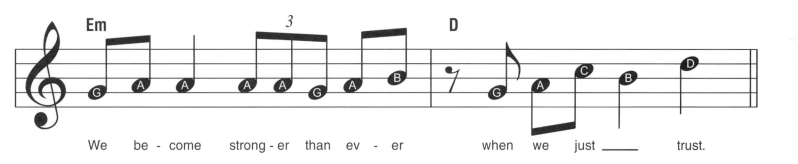

We be - come strong - er than ev - er   when we just _____ trust.

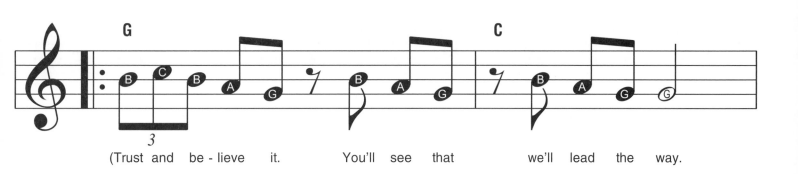

(Trust and be - lieve it.   You'll see that   we'll lead the way.

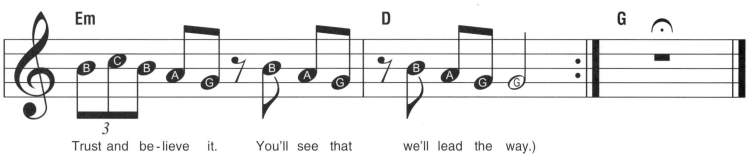

Trust and be - lieve it.   You'll see that   we'll lead the way.)

Les Poissons
from THE LITTLE MERMAID

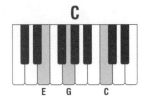
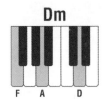
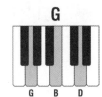
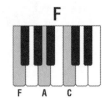
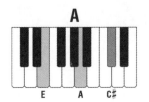

Music by Alan Menken
Lyrics by Howard Ashman

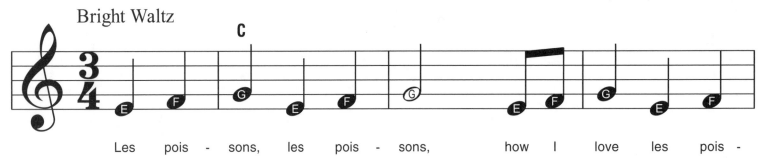

Les pois - sons, les pois - sons, how I love les pois -

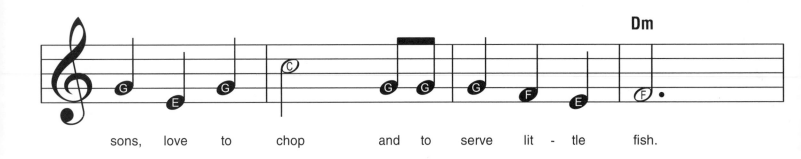

sons, love to chop and to serve lit - tle fish.

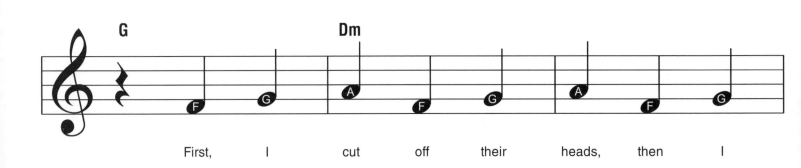

First, I cut off their heads, then I

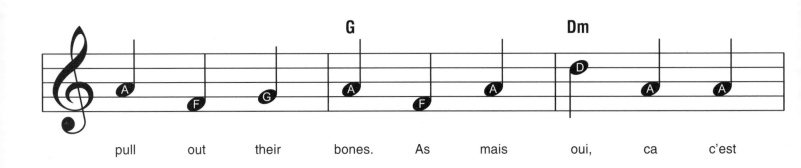

pull out their bones. As mais oui, ca c'est

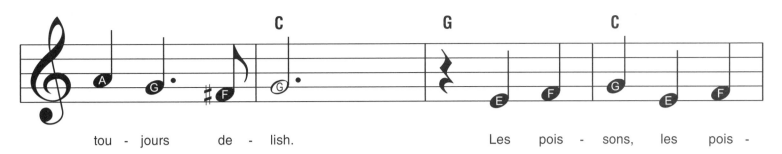

tou - jours de - lish. Les pois - sons, les pois -

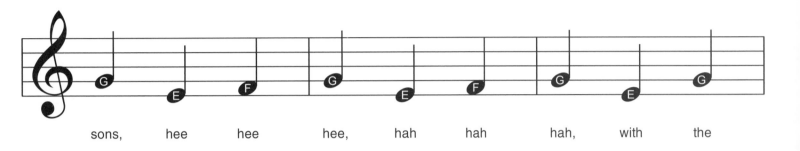

sons, hee hee hee, hah hah hah, with the

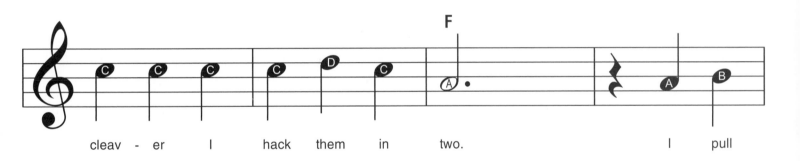

cleav - er I hack them in two. I pull

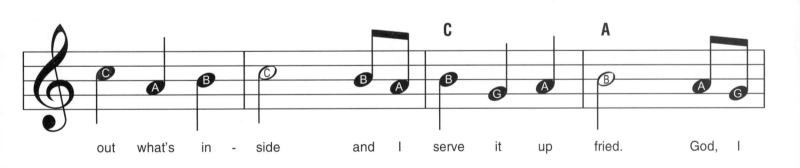

out what's in - side and I serve it up fried. God, I

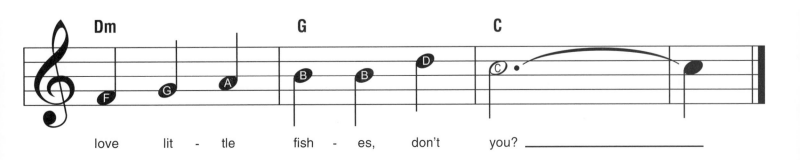

love lit - tle fish - es, don't you? _____

Let's Get Together

from THE PARENT TRAP

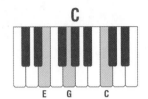
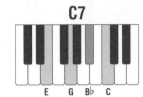
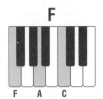

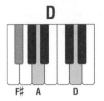

Words and Music by Richard M. Sherman
and Robert B. Sherman

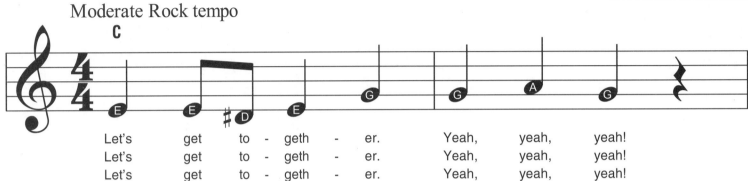

Let's get to-geth-er. Yeah, yeah, yeah!
Let's get to-geth-er. Yeah, yeah, yeah!
Let's get to-geth-er. Yeah, yeah, yeah!

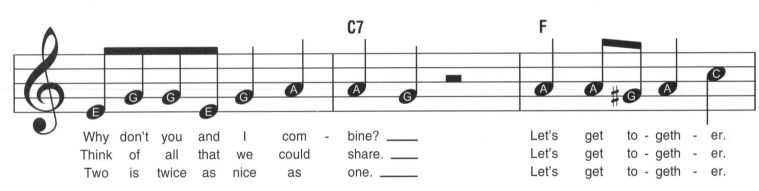

Why don't you and I com-bine? ___ Let's get to-geth-er.
Think of all that we could share. ___ Let's get to-geth-er.
Two is twice as nice as one. ___ Let's get to-geth-er.

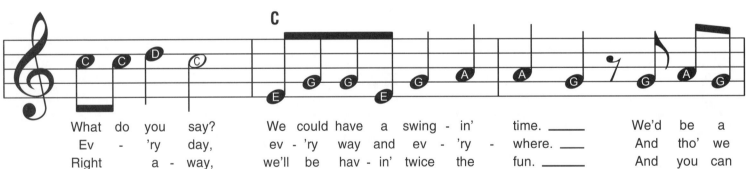

What do you say? We could have a swing-in' time. ___ We'd be a
Ev-'ry day, ev-'ry way and ev-'ry-where. ___ And tho' we
Right a-way, we'll be hav-in' twice the fun. ___ And you can

To Coda

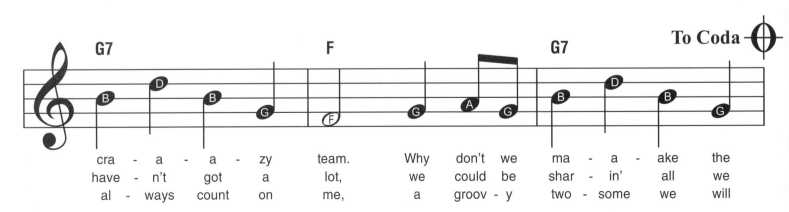

cra - a - a - zy team. Why don't we ma - a - ake the
have - n't got a lot, we could be shar - in' all we
al - ways count on me, a groov-y two - some we will

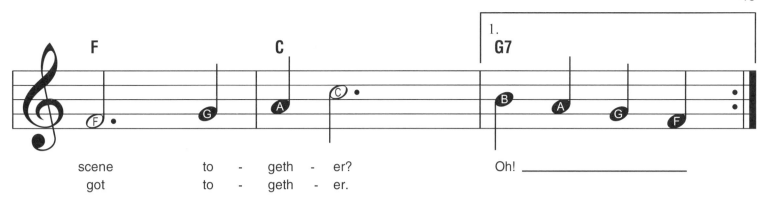

scene to - geth - er?
got to - geth - er.

Oh! _____

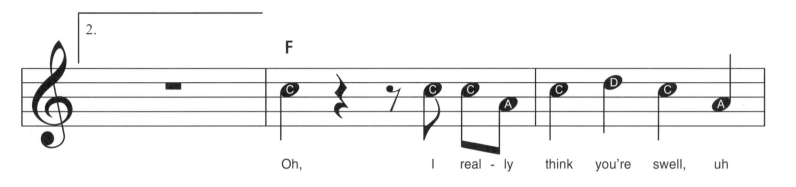

Oh, I real - ly think you're swell, uh

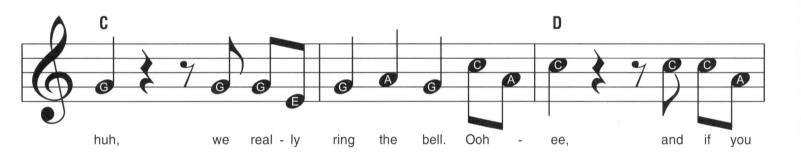

huh, we real - ly ring the bell. Ooh - ee, and if you

D.C. al Coda
(Return to beginning,
play to ⊕ and skip to Coda)

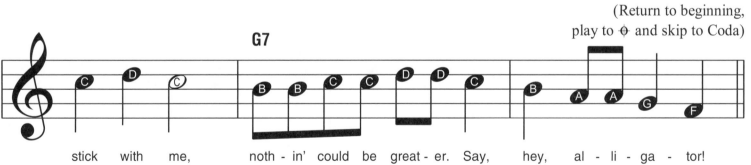

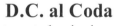

stick with me, noth - in' could be great - er. Say, hey, al - li - ga - tor!

CODA

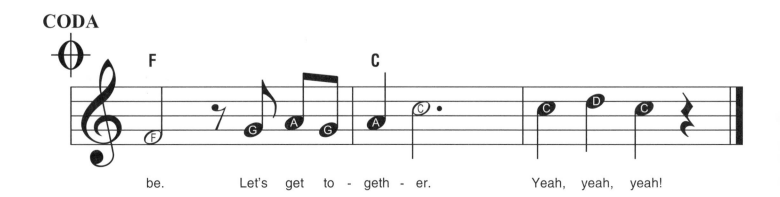

be. Let's get to - geth - er. Yeah, yeah, yeah!

Look Through My Eyes

from BROTHER BEAR

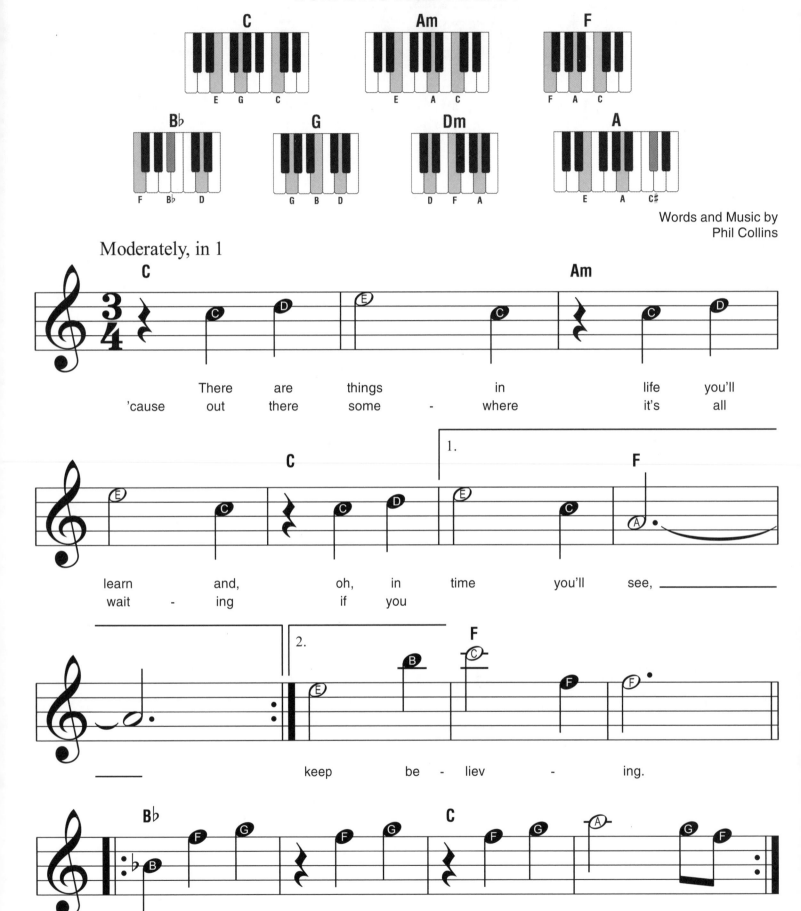

Words and Music by
Phil Collins

Moderately, in 1

There are things in life you'll
'cause out are there some - where it's all

learn and, oh, in time you'll see, _____
wait - ing if you

keep be - liev - ing.

So don't run, don't hide. It will be all _____
right. You'll see; trust me. I'll be there _____

Love Is an Open Door
from FROZEN

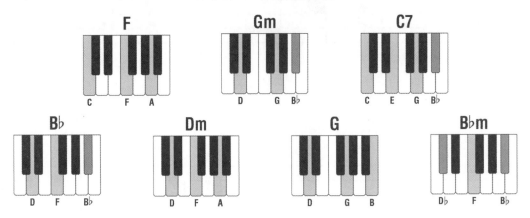

Music and Lyrics by Kristen Anderson-Lopez
and Robert Lopez

Moderately fast

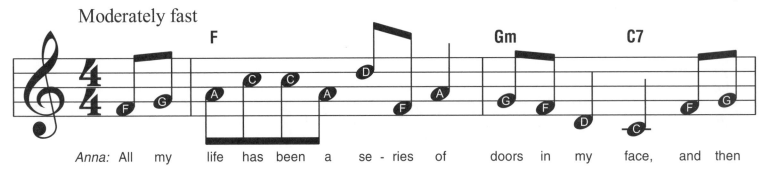

Anna: All my life has been a se - ries of doors in my face, and then

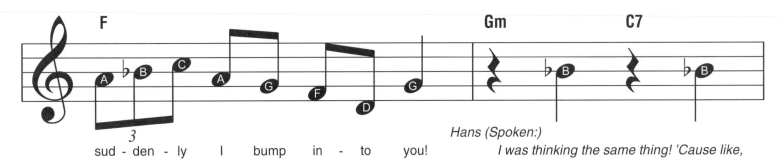

sud - den - ly I bump in - to you!   *Hans (Spoken:)* I was thinking the same thing! 'Cause like,

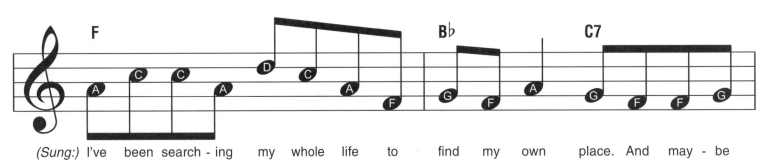

(Sung:) I've been search - ing my whole life to find my own place. And may - be

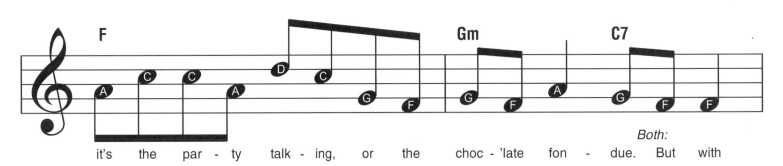

it's the par - ty talk - ing, or the choc - 'late fon - due. But with   *Both:*

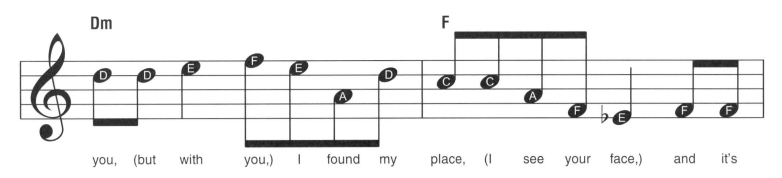

you, (but with you,) I found my place, (I see your face,) and it's

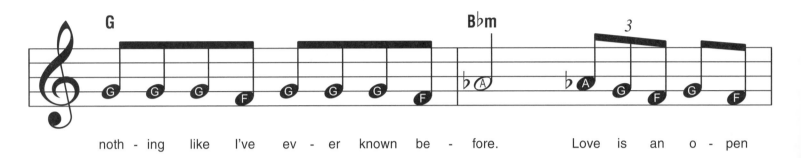

noth - ing like I've ev - er known be - fore. Love is an o - pen

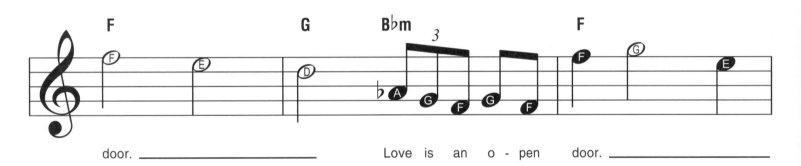

door. _____ Love is an o - pen door. _____

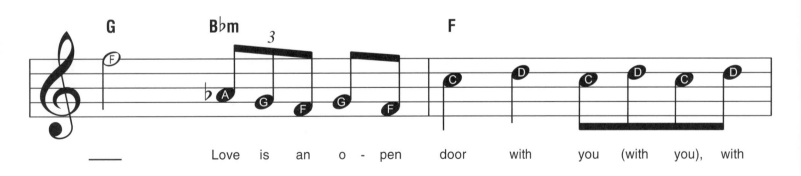

_____ Love is an o - pen door with you (with you), with

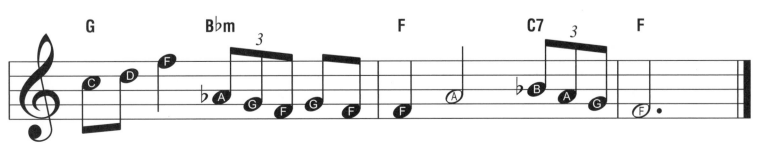

you (with you)! Love is an o - pen door. _____

Loyal Brave True

from MULAN

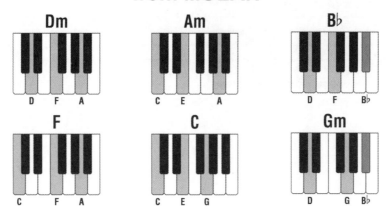

Written by Jamie Hartman,
Billy Crabtree, Rosi Golan
and Harry Gregson-Williams

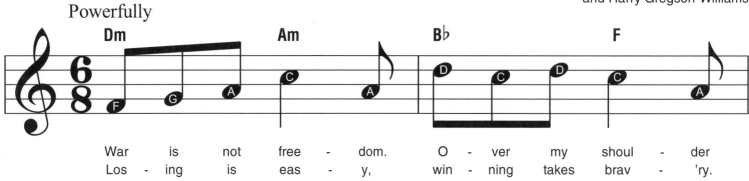

War is not free - dom. O - ver my shoul - der
Los - ing is eas - y, win - ning takes brav - 'ry.

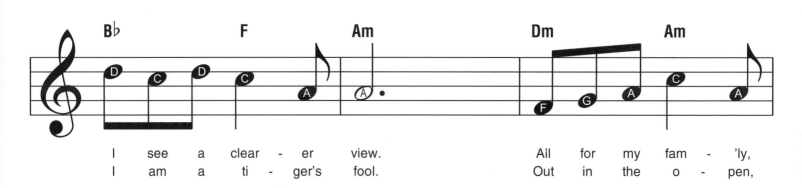

I see a clear - er view. All for my fam - 'ly,
I am a ti - ger's fool. Out in the o - pen,

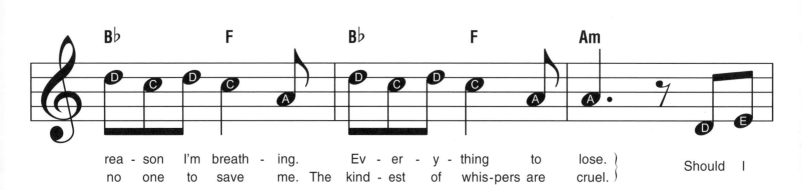

rea - son I'm breath - ing. Ev - er - y - thing to lose.)
no one to save me. The kind - est of whis-pers are cruel.)

Should I

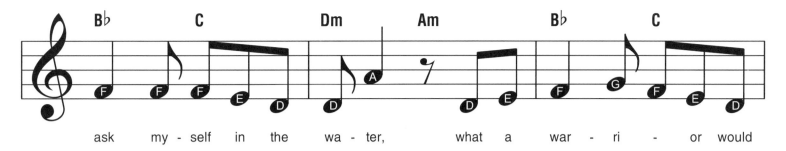

ask my - self in the wa - ter, what a war - ri - or would

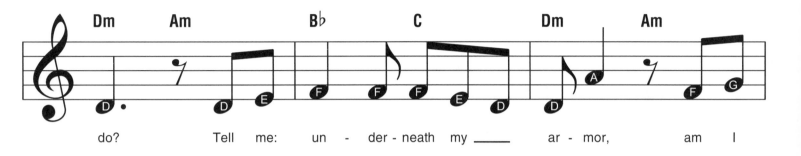

do? Tell me: un - der - neath my _____ ar - mor, am I

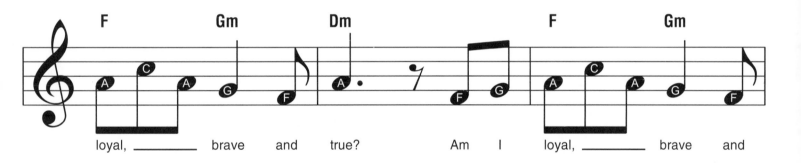

loyal, _____ brave and true? Am I loyal, _____ brave and

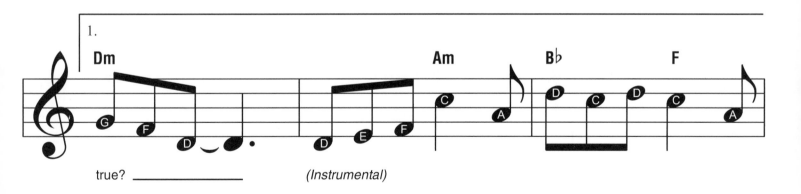

true? _____ (Instrumental)

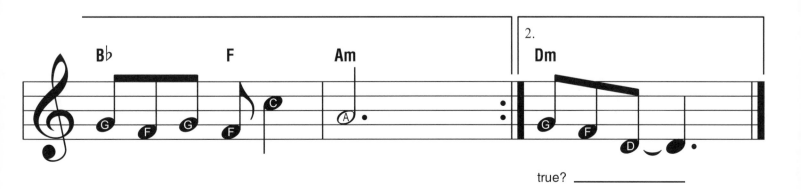

true? _____

Nobody Like U
from TURNING RED

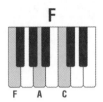
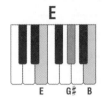

Music and Lyrics by Billie Eilish
and Finneas O'Connell

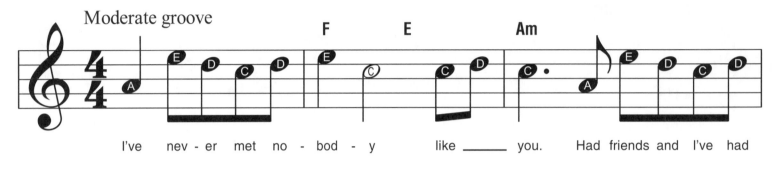

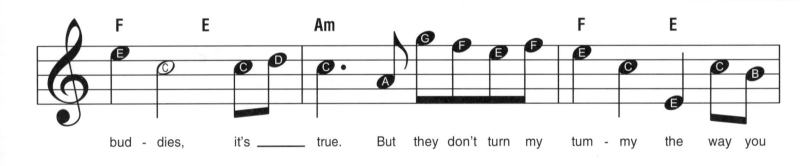

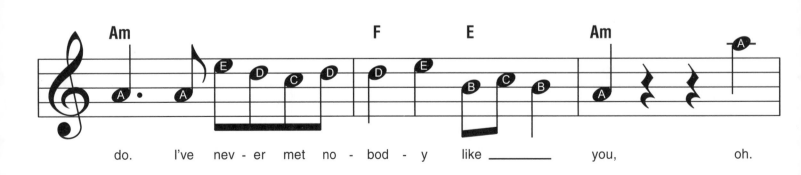

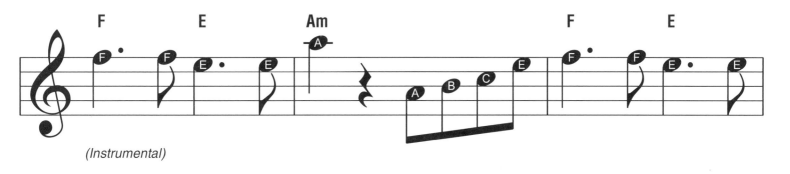

(Instrumental)

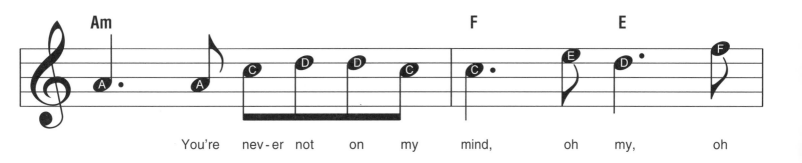

You're nev - er not on my mind, oh my, oh

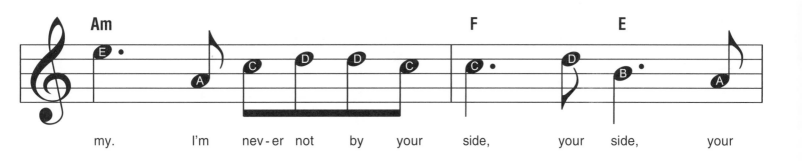

my. I'm nev - er not by your side, your side, your

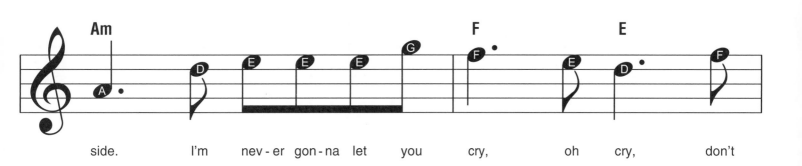

side. I'm nev - er gon - na let you cry, oh cry, don't

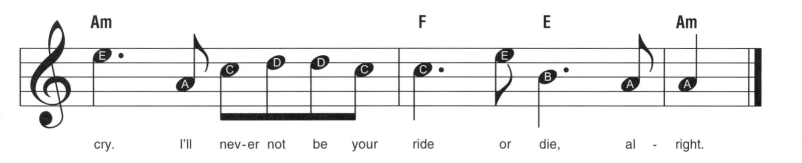

cry. I'll nev - er not be your ride or die, al - right.

Once Upon a Dream
from SLEEPING BEAUTY

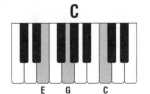
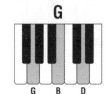
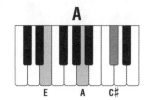

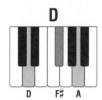

Words and Music by Sammy Fain
and Jack Lawrence
Adapted from a theme by Tchaikovsky

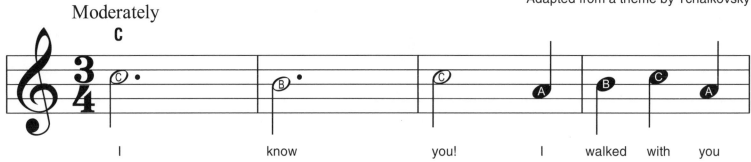

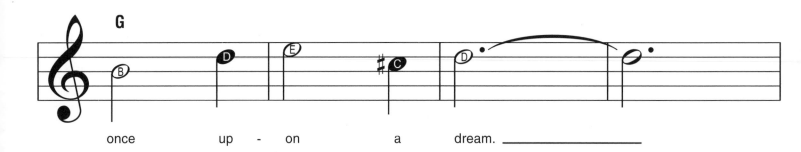

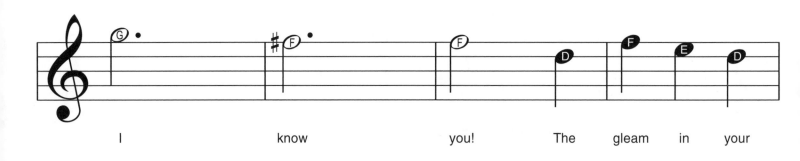

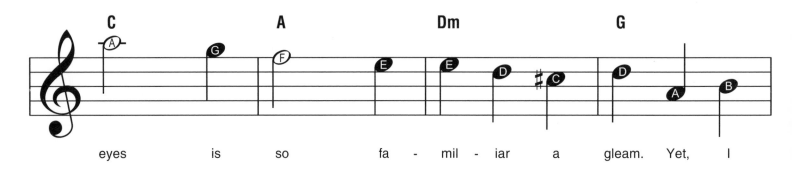

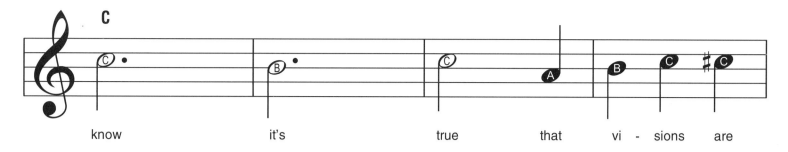

know   it's   true   that   vi - sions   are

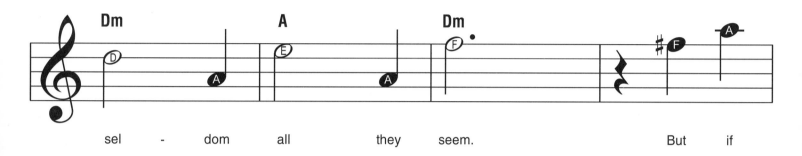

sel - dom   all   they   seem.   But   if

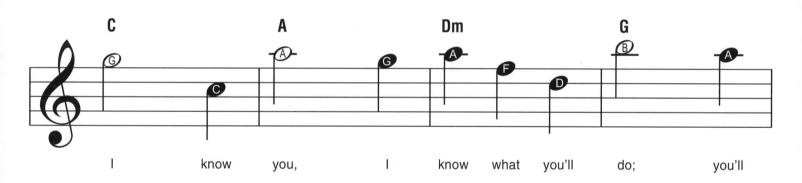

I   know   you,   I   know   what you'll   do;   you'll

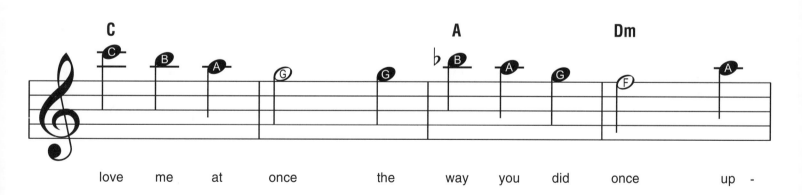

love   me   at   once   the   way   you   did   once   up -

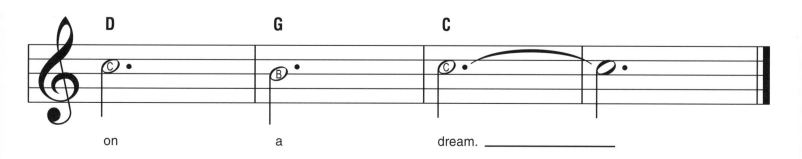

on   a   dream. _____

The Place Where Lost Things Go

from MARY POPPINS RETURNS

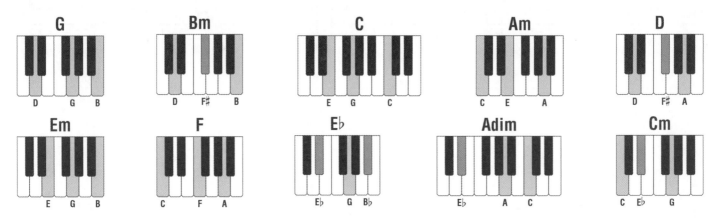

Music by Marc Shaiman
Lyrics by Scott Wittman and Marc Shaiman

Gently, not slow

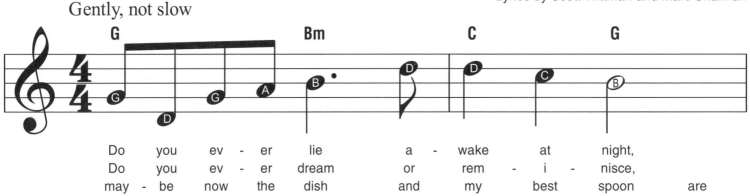

Do you ev - er lie a - wake at night,
Do you ev - er dream or rem - i - nisce,
may - be now the dish and my best spoon are

To Coda

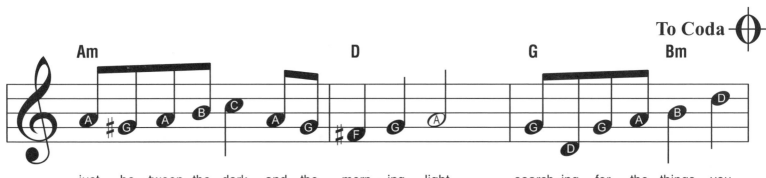

just be - tween the dark and the morn - ing light, search-ing for the things you
won - d'ring where to find what you tru - ly miss? Well, may - be all those things that
play - ing hide and seek just be - hind the moon, wait - ing there un - til it's

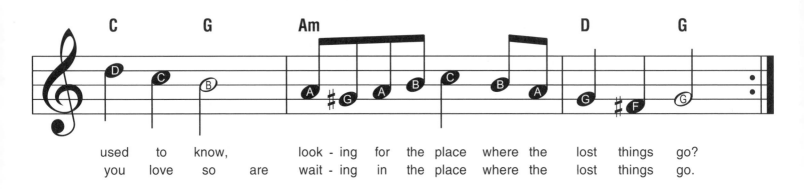

used to know, look - ing for the place where the lost things go?
you love so are wait - ing in the place where the lost things go.

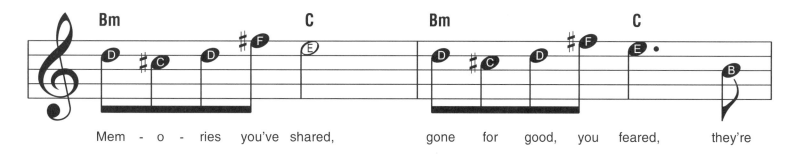

Mem - o - ries you've shared, gone for good, you feared, they're

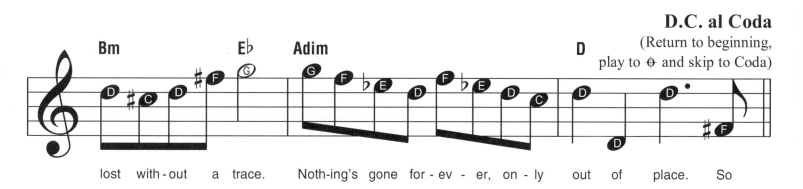

all a - round you still, though they've dis - ap - peared. Noth - ing's real - ly left, or

D.C. al Coda
(Return to beginning,
play to ⊕ and skip to Coda)

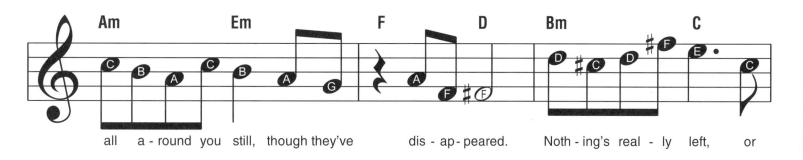

lost with - out a trace. Noth - ing's gone for - ev - er, on - ly out of place. So

CODA

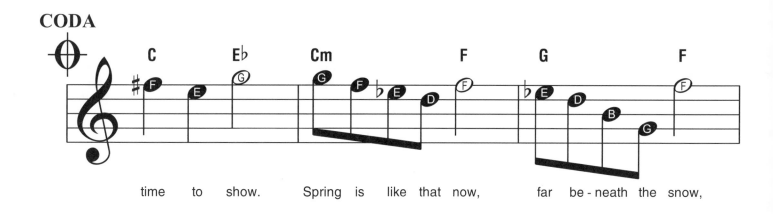

time to show. Spring is like that now, far be - neath the snow,

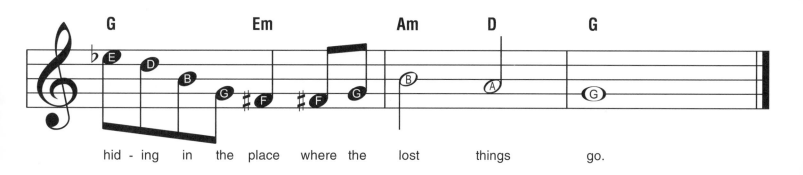

hid - ing in the place where the lost things go.

Queen of Mean

from DESCENDANTS 3

 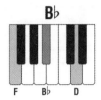 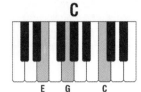 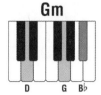

Written by Antonina Armato,
Tim James, Thomas Sturges
and Adam Schmalholz

Moderately

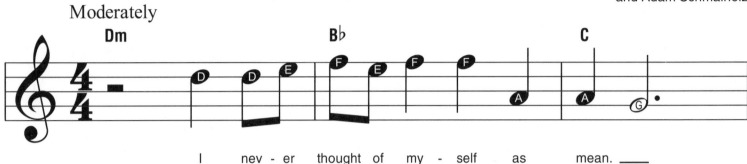

I nev-er thought of my-self as mean. ___

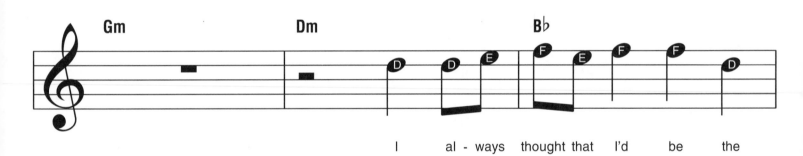

I al-ways thought that I'd be the

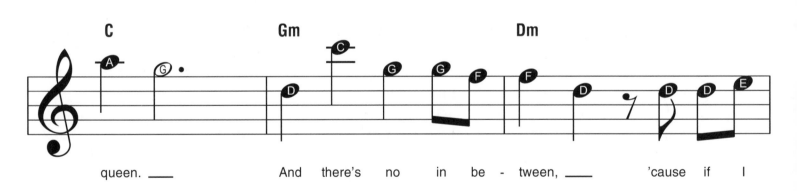

queen. ___ And there's no in be-tween, ___ 'cause if I

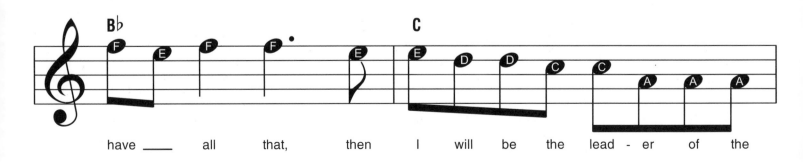

have ___ all that, then I will be the lead-er of the

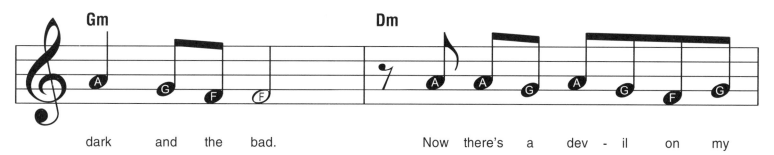

dark   and   the   bad.   Now   there's   a   dev - il   on   my

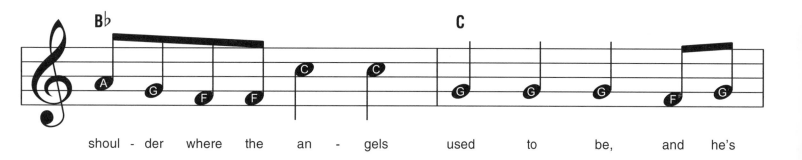

shoul - der   where   the   an - gels   used   to   be,   and   he's

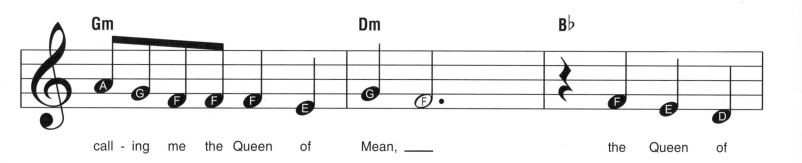

call - ing   me   the   Queen   of   Mean, ____   the   Queen   of

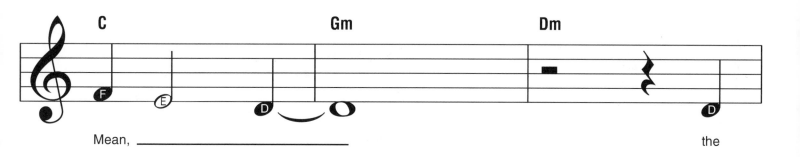

Mean, _____   the

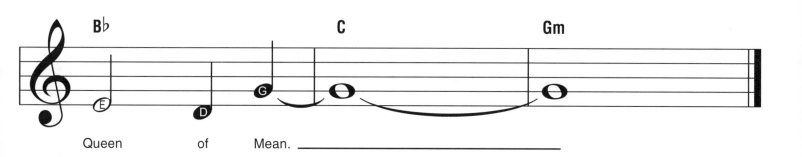

Queen   of   Mean. _____

Reindeer(s) Are Better Than People
from FROZEN

Music and Lyrics by Kristen Anderson-Lopez
and Robert Lopez

65

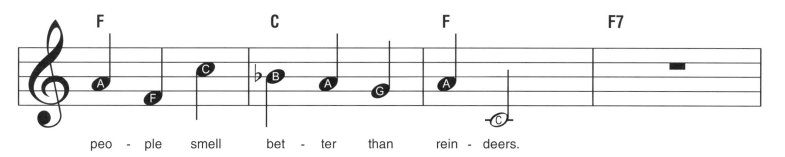

peo - ple smell bet - ter than rein - deers.

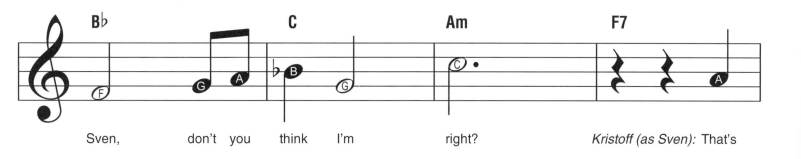

Sven, don't you think I'm right? *Kristoff (as Sven):* That's

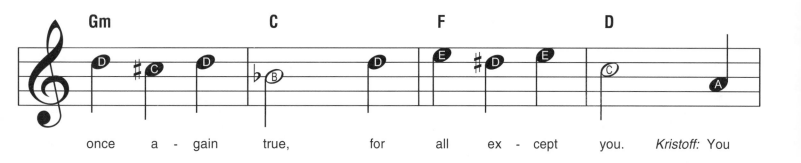

once a - gain true, for all ex - cept you. *Kristoff:* You

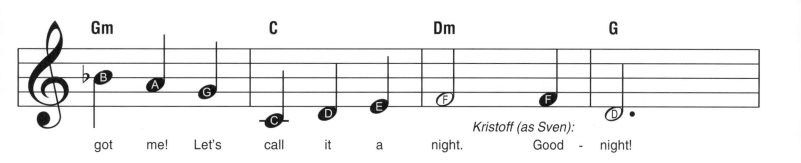

got me! Let's call it a night. *Kristoff (as Sven):* Good - night!

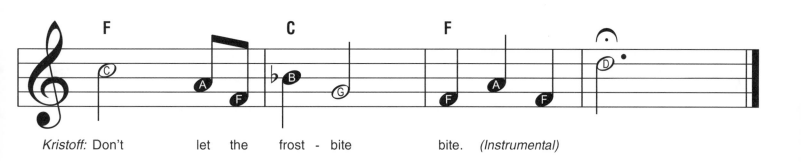

Kristoff: Don't let the frost - bite bite. *(Instrumental)*

Remember Me
(Ernesto de la Cruz)
from COCO

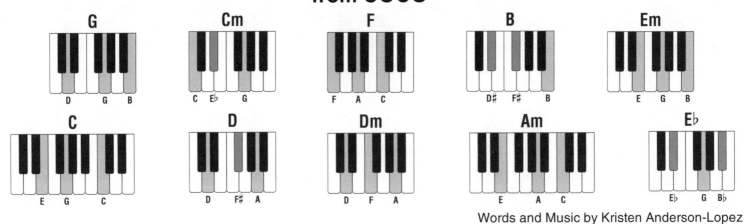

Words and Music by Kristen Anderson-Lopez
and Robert Lopez

Moderately fast

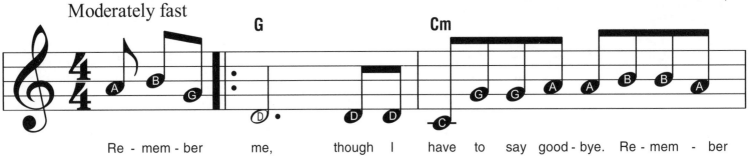

Re - mem - ber me, though I have to say good - bye. Re - mem - ber

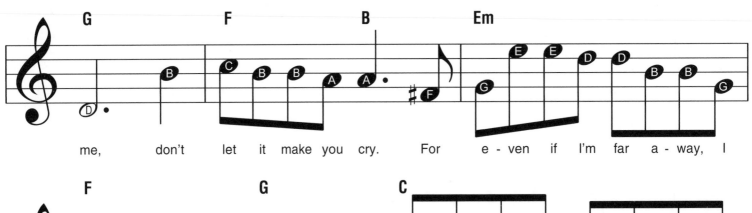

me, don't let it make you cry. For e - ven if I'm far a - way, I

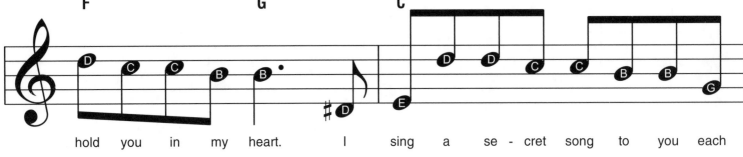

hold you in my heart. I sing a se - cret song to you each

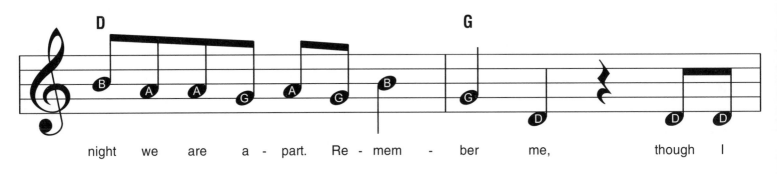

night we are a - part. Re - mem - ber me, though I

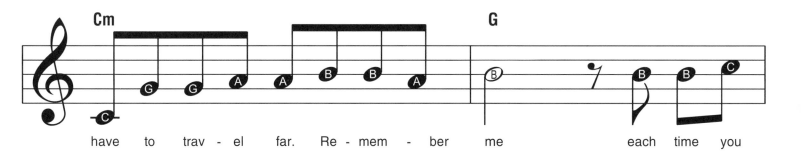

have to trav - el far. Re - mem - ber me each time you

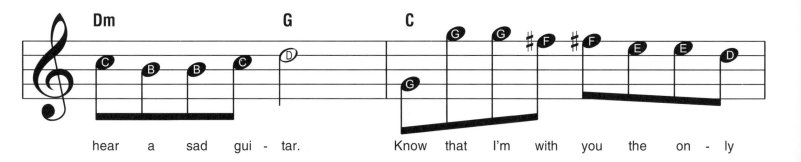

hear a sad gui - tar. Know that I'm with you the on - ly

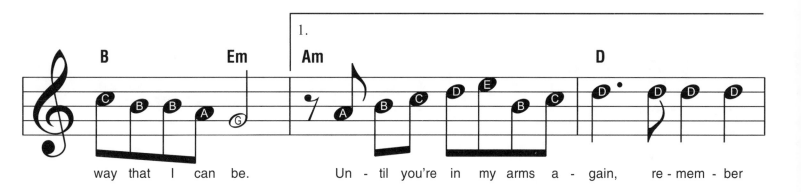

1.

way that I can be. Un - til you're in my arms a - gain, re - mem - ber

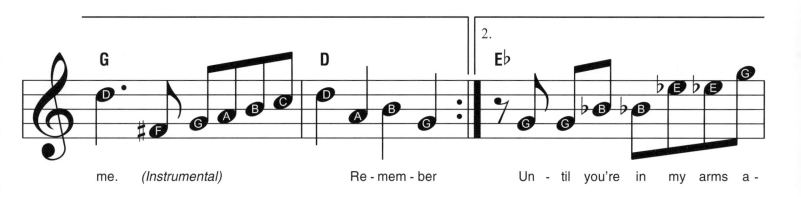

2.

me. *(Instrumental)* Re - mem - ber Un - til you're in my arms a -

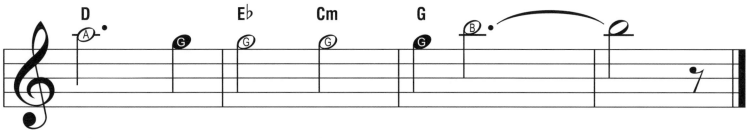

gain, re - mem - ber me. _____

The Rose Song
from HIGH SCHOOL MUSICAL: THE MUSICAL: THE SERIES (SEASON 2)

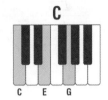
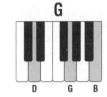

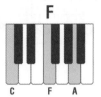

Music and Lyrics by
Olivia Rodrigo

Piano Ballad

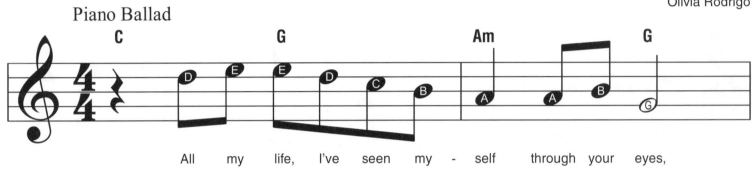

All my life, I've seen my-self through your eyes,

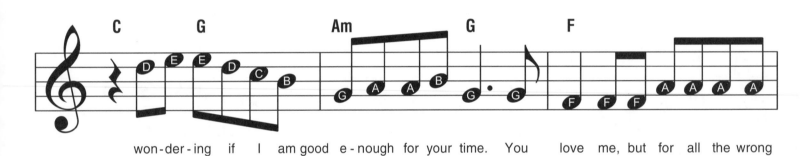

won-der-ing if I am good e-nough for your time. You love me, but for all the wrong

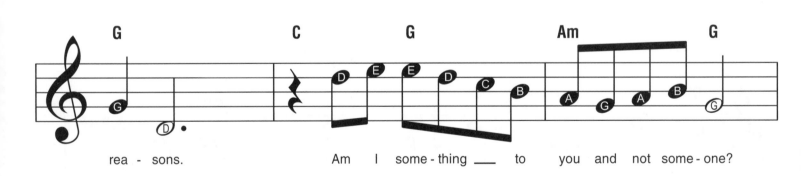

rea-sons. Am I some-thing ___ to you and not some-one?

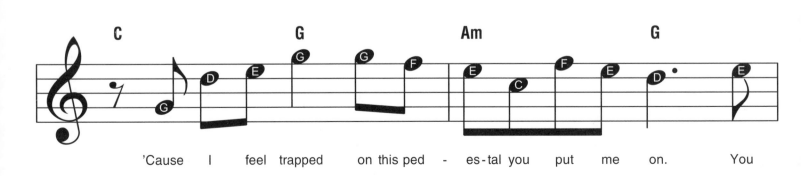

'Cause I feel trapped on this ped-es-tal you put me on. You

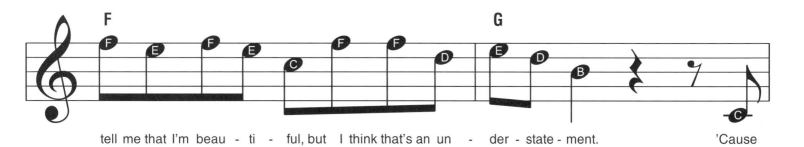

tell me that I'm beau - ti - ful, but I think that's an un - - der - state - ment. 'Cause

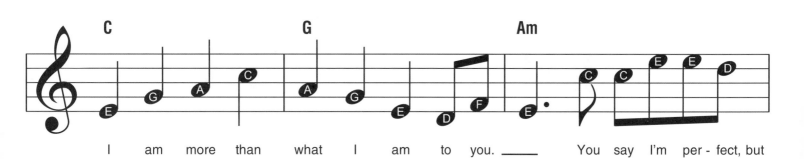

I am more than what I am to you. _____ You say I'm per - fect, but

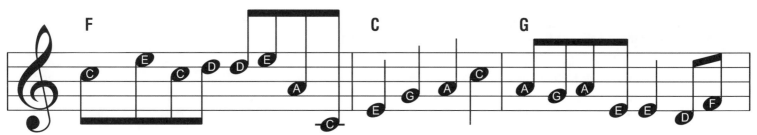

I've got thorns with my pet - als, too. And I won't be con - fined to your __ point of view. __

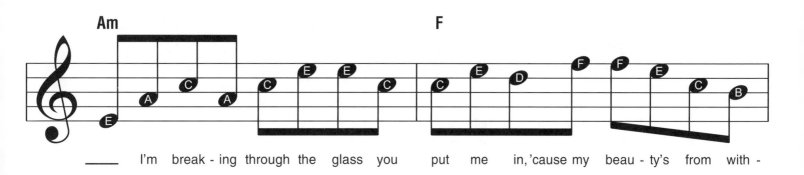

__ I'm break - ing through the glass you put me in, 'cause my beau - ty's from with -

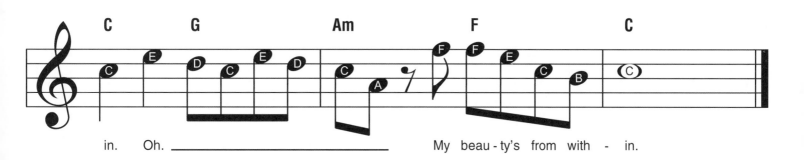

in. Oh. _____ My beau - ty's from with - in.

Seize the Day
from NEWSIES THE MUSICAL

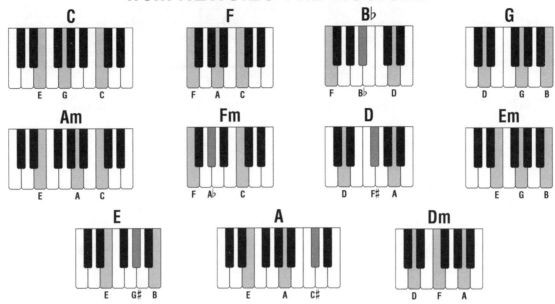

Music by Alan Menken
Lyrics by Jack Feldman

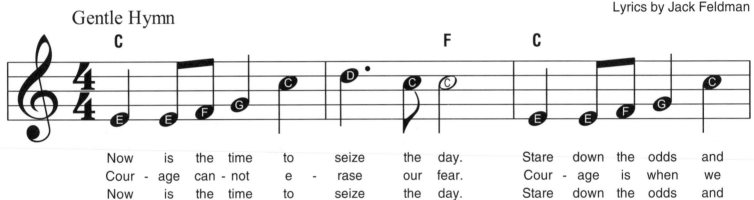

Now is the time to seize the day. Stare down the odds and
Cour - age can - not e - rase our fear. Cour - age is when we
Now is the time to seize the day. Stare down the odds and

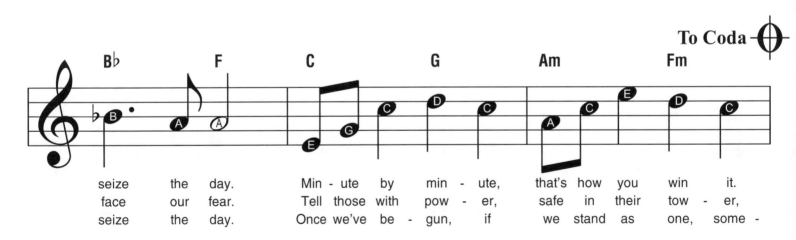

seize the day. Min - ute by min - ute, that's how you win it.
face our fear. Tell those with pow - er, safe in their tow - er,
seize the day. Once we've be - gun, if we stand as one, some -

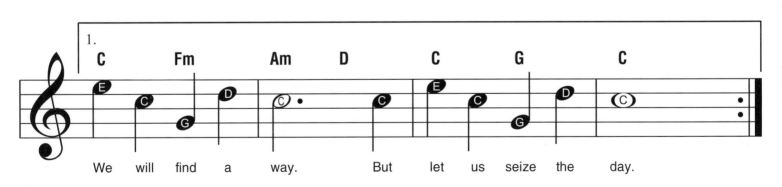

We will find a way. But let us seize the day.

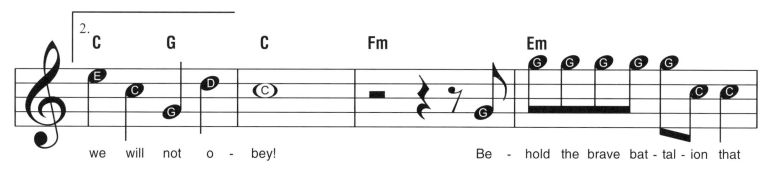

2.

| C | G | C | Fm | Em |

we will not o - bey!   Be - hold the brave bat - tal - ion that

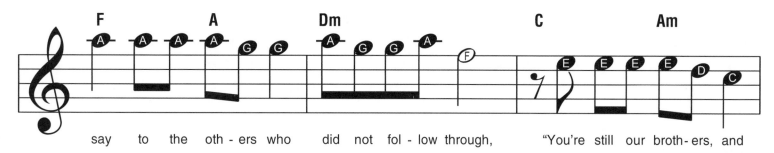

| F | Em | Am | E | C |

stands side by side,   too few in num - ber and   too proud to hide.   Then

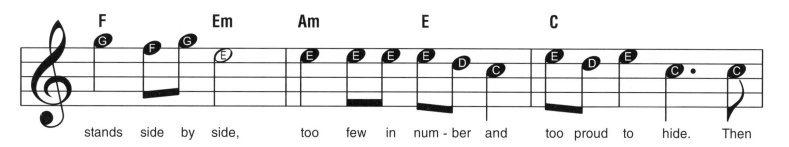

| F | A | Dm | C | Am |

say to the oth - ers who did not fol - low through,   "You're still our broth - ers, and

D.C. al Coda
(Return to beginning,
play to ⊕ and skip to Coda)

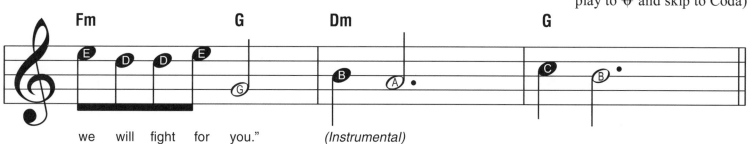

| Fm | G | Dm | G |

we will fight for you."   *(Instrumental)*

CODA

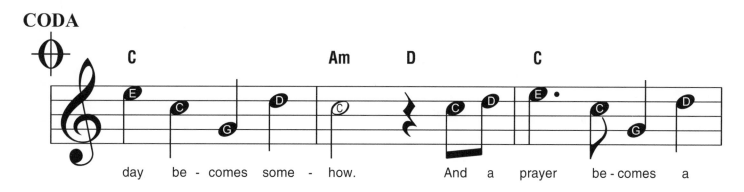

| C | Am | D | C |

day be - comes some - how.   And a prayer be - comes a

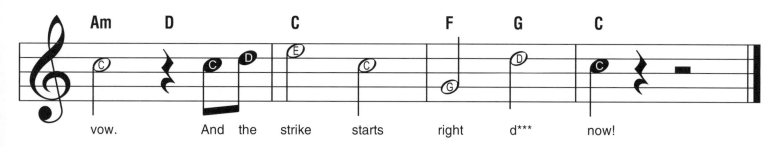

| Am | D | C | F | G | C |

vow.   And the strike starts right d*** now!

Show Yourself
from FROZEN 2

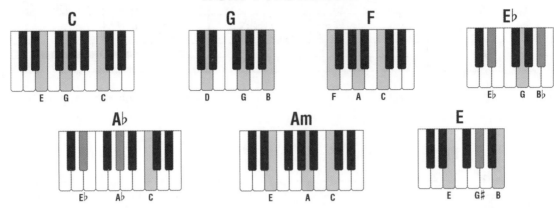

Music and Lyrics by Kristen Anderson-Lopez
and Robert Lopez

Moderately

Ev - 'ry inch of me is trem - bling, but not from the cold. _____

_____ Some-thing is fa - mil - iar, like a dream I can

reach, but not quite hold. I can sense you there,

like a friend I've al - ways known. _____ I'm ar -

riv - ing, and it feels like I am home. _____

So Close
from ENCHANTED

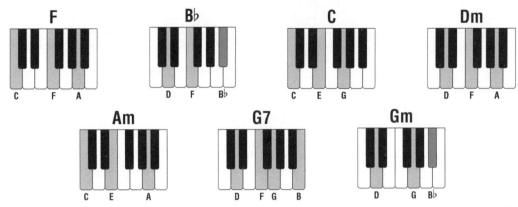

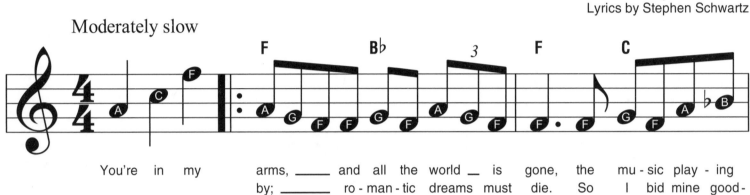

Music by Alan Menken
Lyrics by Stephen Schwartz

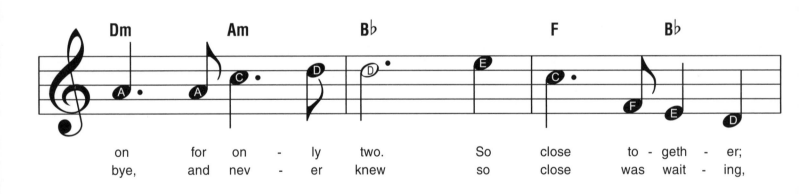

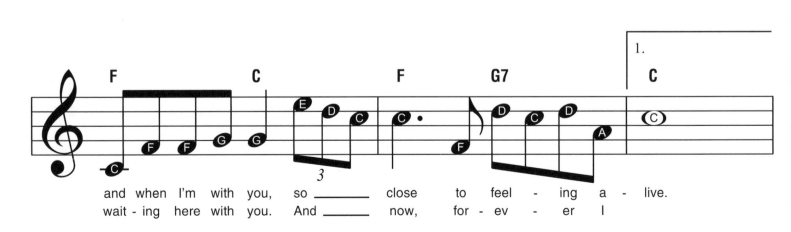

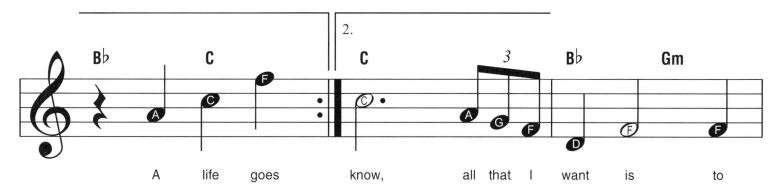

A life goes know, all that I want is to

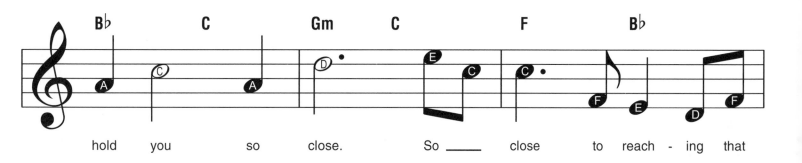

hold you so close. So ____ close to reach - ing that

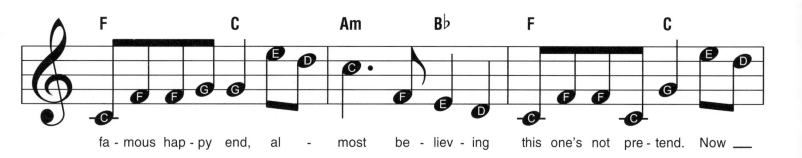

fa - mous hap - py end, al - most be - liev - ing this one's not pre - tend. Now ___

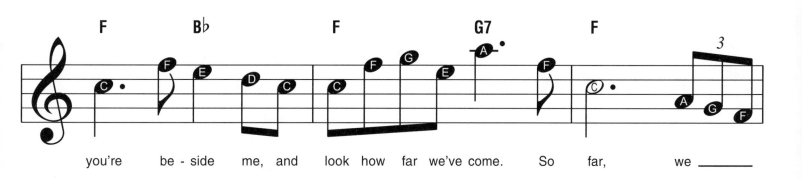

you're be - side me, and look how far we've come. So far, we ____

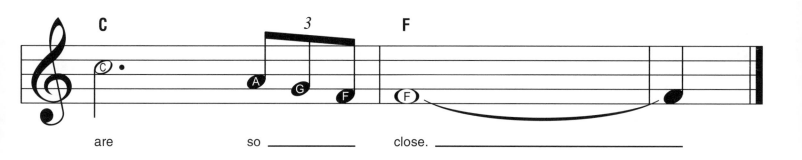

are so ____ close. ____

Speechless

from ALADDIN

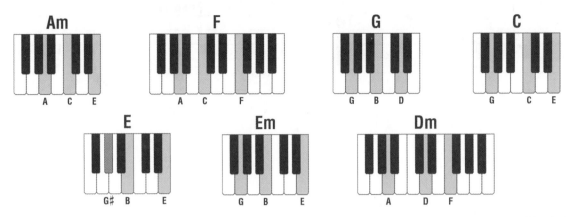

Music by Alan Menken
Lyrics by Benj Pasek and Justin Paul

Half-time feel

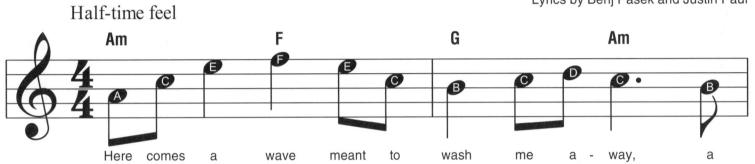

Here comes a wave meant to wash me a - way, a

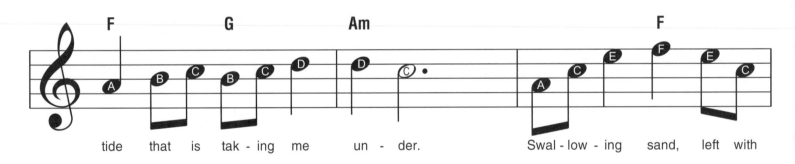

tide that is tak - ing me un - der. Swal - low - ing sand, left with

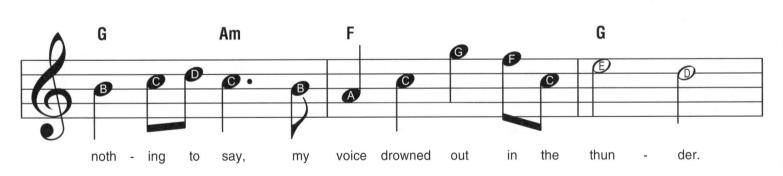

noth - ing to say, my voice drowned out in the thun - der.

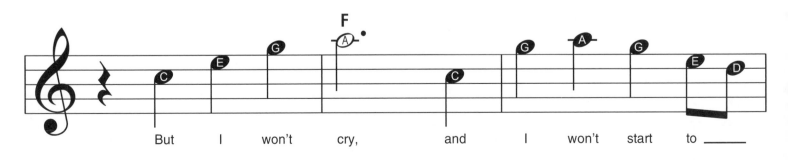

But I won't cry, and I won't start to _____

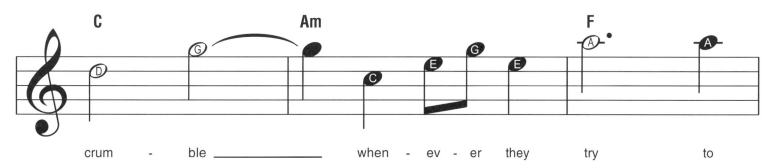

crum - ble _____ when - ev - er they try to

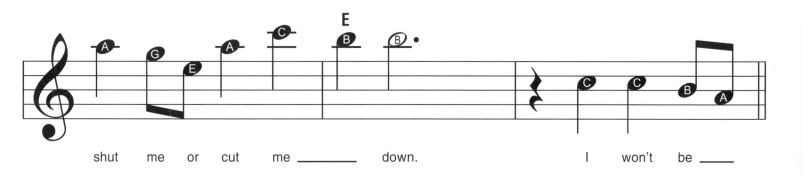

shut me or cut me _____ down. I won't be ____

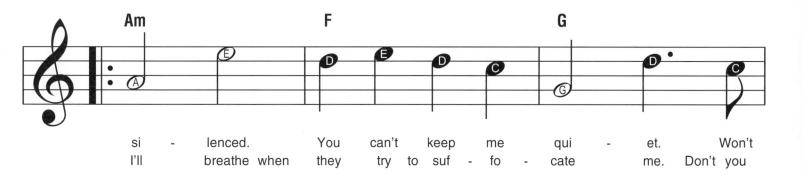

si - lenced. You can't keep me qui - et. Won't
I'll breathe when they try to suf - fo - cate me. Don't you

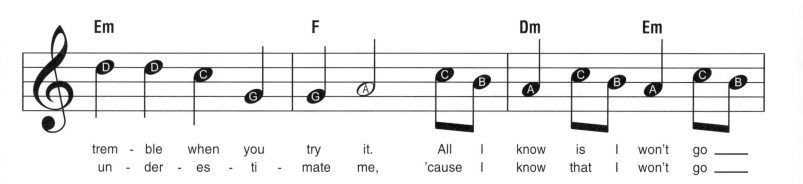

trem - ble when you try it. All I know is I won't go ____
un - der - es - ti - mate me, 'cause I know that I won't go ____

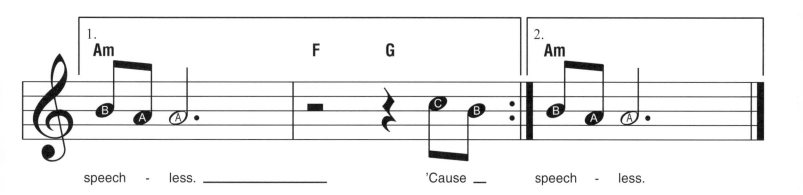

speech - less. _____ 'Cause __ speech - less.

Spirit
from THE LION KING (2019)

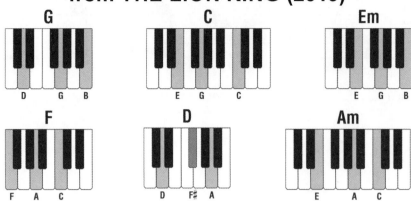

Written by Timothy McKenzie,
Ilya Salmanzadeh and Beyoncé

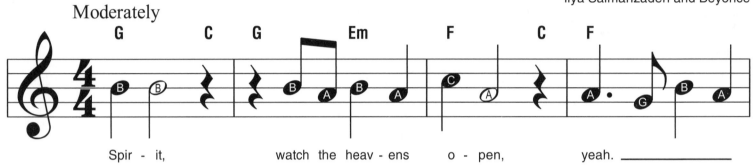

Moderately

Spir - it, watch the heav - ens o - pen, yeah. _____

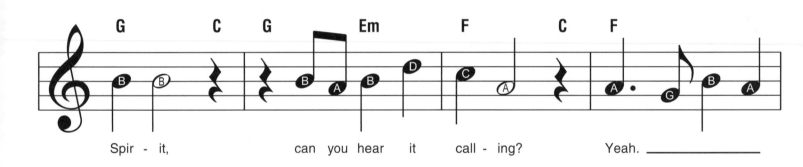

Spir - it, can you hear it call - ing? Yeah. _____

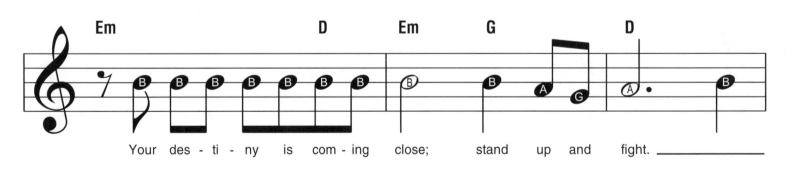

Your des - ti - ny is com - ing close; stand up and fight. _____

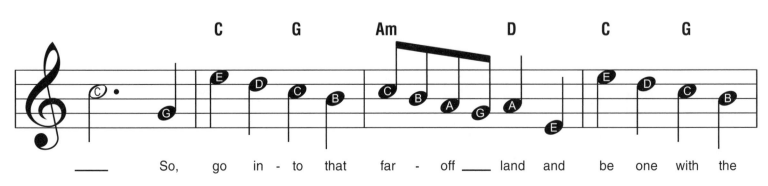

_____ So, go in - to that far - off _____ land and be one with the

Surface Pressure
from ENCANTO

 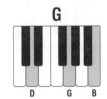 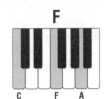 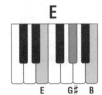 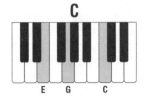

Music and Lyrics by
Lin-Manuel Miranda

Moderate Pop

Un - der the sur - face, I feel ber-serk as a tight - rope walk - er in a

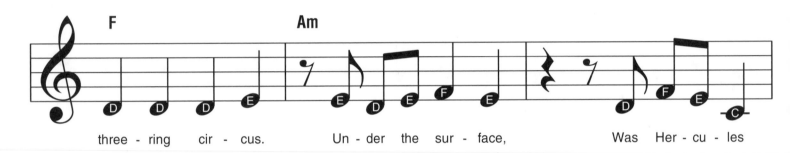

three - ring cir - cus. Un - der the sur - face, Was Her - cu - les

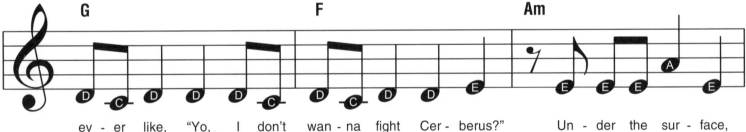

ev - er like, "Yo, I don't wan - na fight Cer - berus?" Un - der the sur - face,

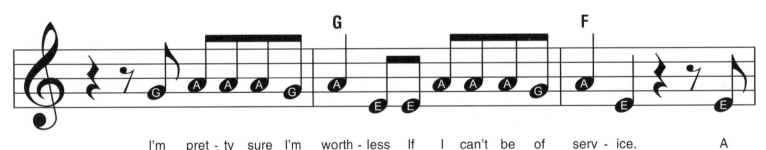

I'm pret - ty sure I'm worth - less If I can't be of serv - ice. A

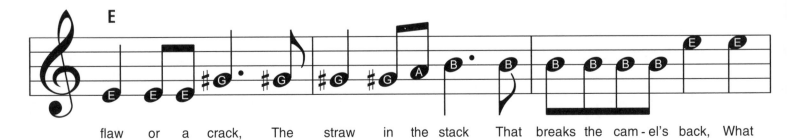

flaw or a crack, The straw in the stack That breaks the cam - el's back, What

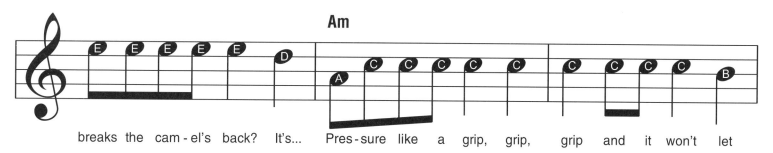

breaks the cam-el's back? It's... Pres-sure like a grip, grip, grip and it won't let

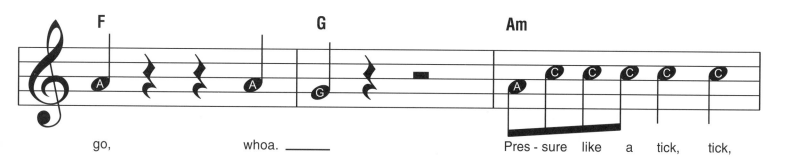

go, whoa. _____ Pres-sure like a tick, tick,

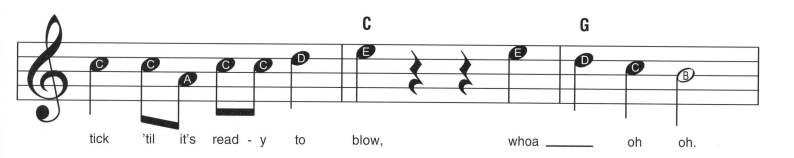

tick 'til it's read-y to blow, whoa _____ oh oh.

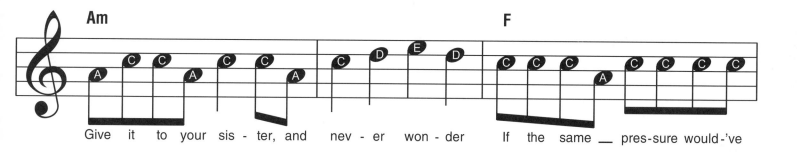

Give it to your sis-ter, and nev-er won-der If the same _ pres-sure would-'ve

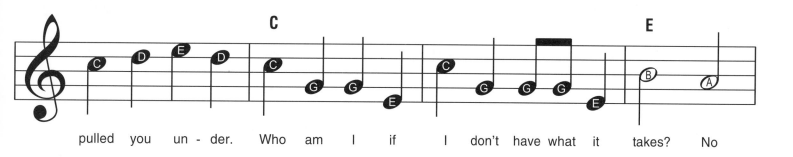

pulled you un-der. Who am I if I don't have what it takes? No

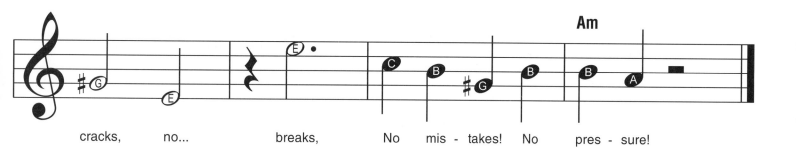

cracks, no... breaks, No mis-takes! No pres-sure!

Trust in Me
(The Python's Song)
from THE JUNGLE BOOK

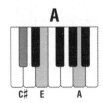
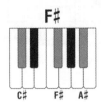
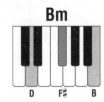
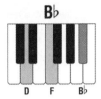

Words and Music by Richard M. Sherman
and Robert B. Sherman

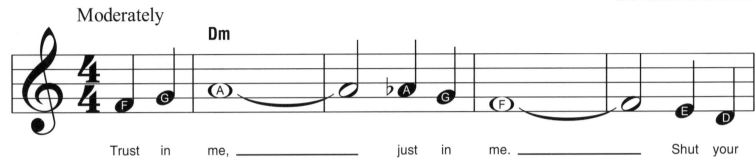

Trust in me, _____ just in me. _____ Shut your

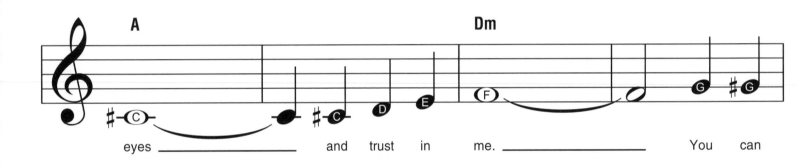

eyes _____ and trust in me. _____ You can

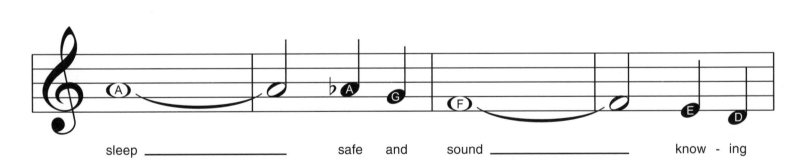

sleep _____ safe and sound _____ know - ing

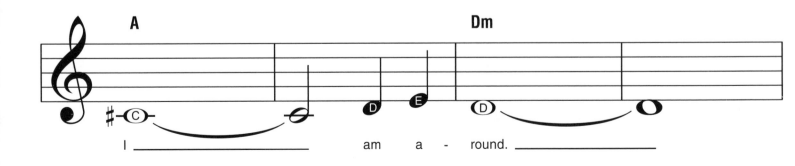

I _____ am a - round. _____

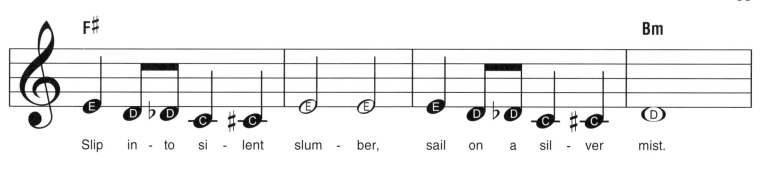

Slip in - to si - lent slum - ber, sail on a sil - ver mist.

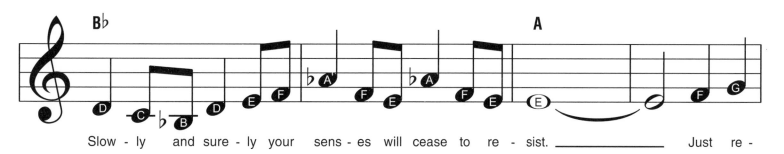

Slow - ly and sure - ly your sens - es will cease to re - sist. Just re -

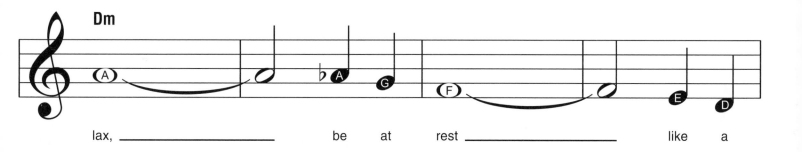

lax, be at rest like a

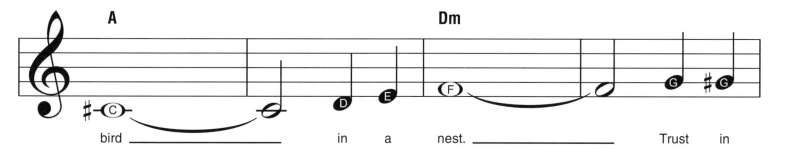

bird in a nest. Trust in

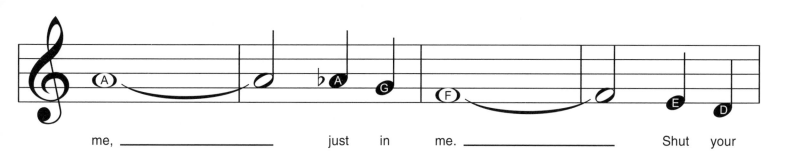

me, just in me. Shut your

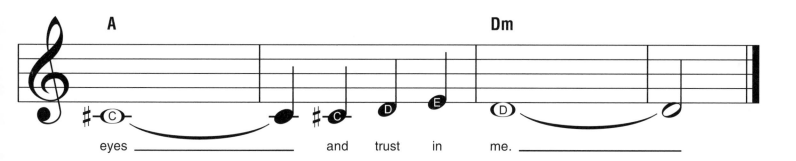

eyes and trust in me.

Un Poco Loco
from COCO

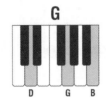
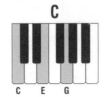
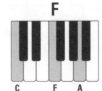

Music by Germaine Franco
Lyrics by Adrian Molina

Moderately, in 2, with a bounce

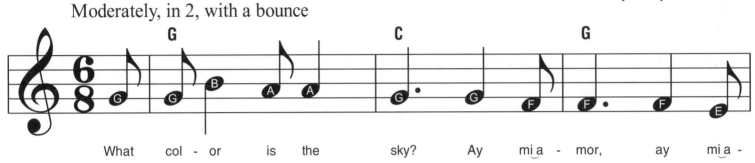

What col- or is the sky? Ay mi a - mor, ay mi a -

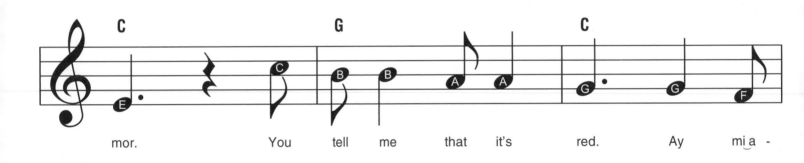

mor. You tell me that it's red. Ay mi a -

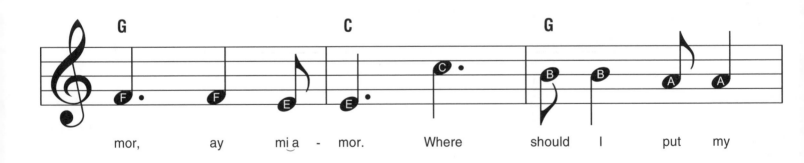

mor, ay mi a - mor. Where should I put my

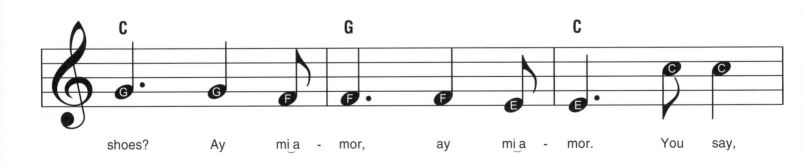

shoes? Ay mi a - mor, ay mi a - mor. You say,

We Don't Talk About Bruno
from ENCANTO

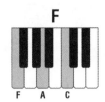
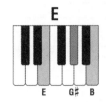
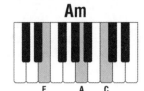
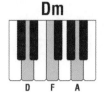

Music and Lyrics by
Lin-Manuel Miranda

Moderately

Pepa: We don't talk a - bout Bru - no, no, no, no!

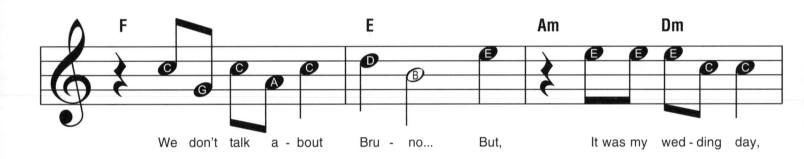

We don't talk a - bout Bru - no... But, It was my wed - ding day,

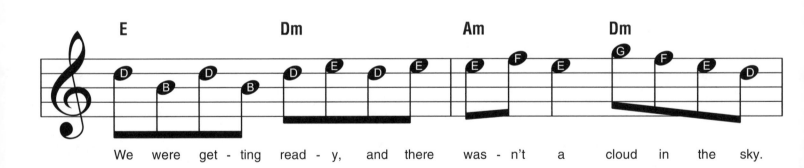

We were get - ting read - y, and there was - n't a cloud in the sky.

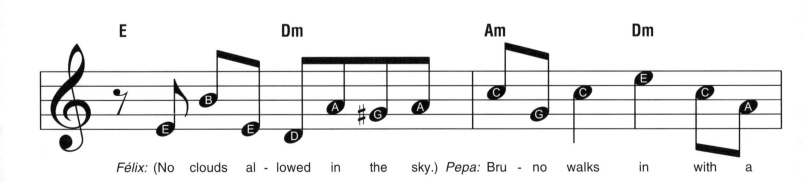

Félix: (No clouds al - lowed in the sky.) *Pepa:* Bru - no walks in with a

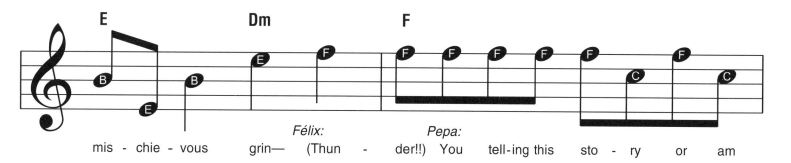

mis - chie - vous grin— (Thun - der!!) You tell-ing this sto - ry or am

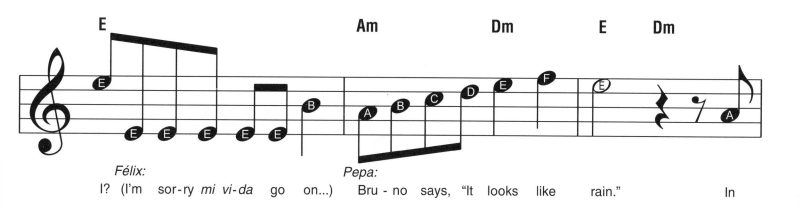

Félix: I? (I'm sor-ry *mi vi-da* go on...) *Pepa:* Bru - no says, "It looks like rain." In

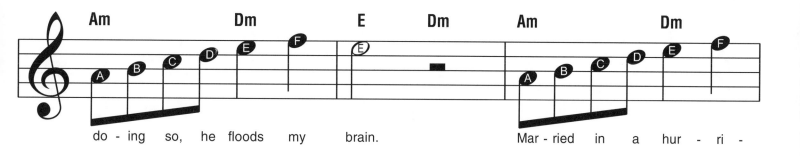

do - ing so, he floods my brain. Mar - ried in a hur - ri -

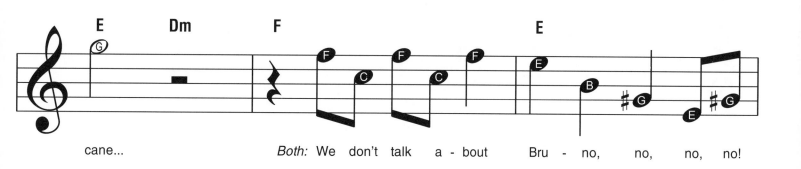

cane... *Both:* We don't talk a - bout Bru - no, no, no, no!

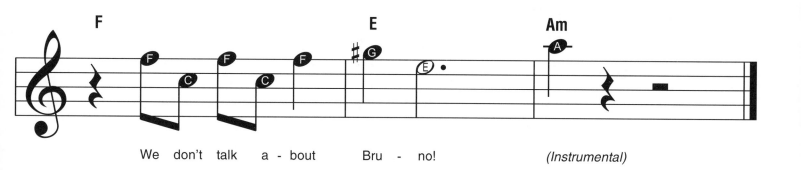

We don't talk a - bout Bru - no! *(Instrumental)*

When Will My Life Begin?

from TANGLED

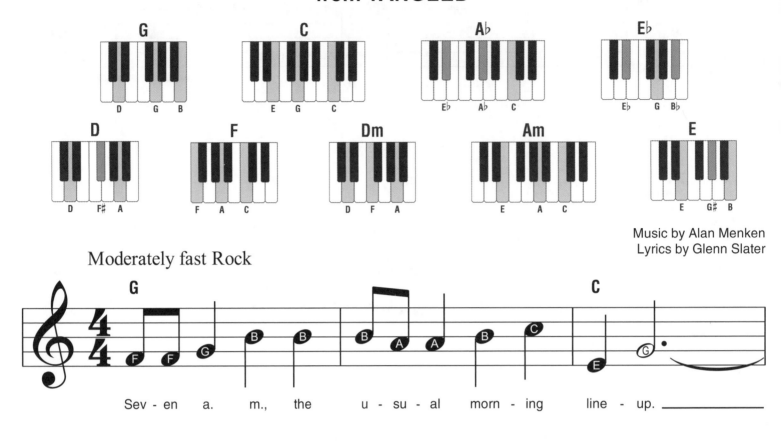

Music by Alan Menken
Lyrics by Glenn Slater

Moderately fast Rock

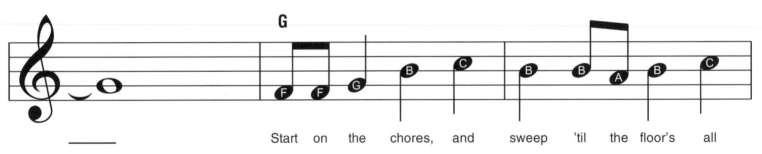

Sev - en a. m., the u - su - al morn - ing line - up. _____

_____ Start on the chores, and sweep 'til the floor's all clean. _____ Pol - ish and wax, do

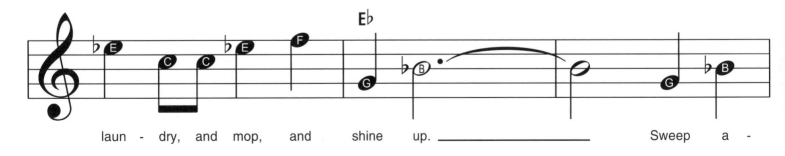

laun - dry, and mop, and shine up. _____ Sweep a -

You Can't Stop the Girl

from MALEFICENT: MISTRESS OF EVIL

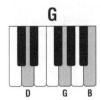
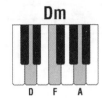
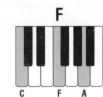

G   Dm   F   C

Words and Music by Bleta Rexha,
Nate Cyphert, Michael Pollack,
Alex Schwartz, Joe Khajadourian,
Sean Nelson, Jeff J. Lin,
Evan Sult and Aaron Huffman

Moderate half-time feel

Oh,   they're tryin' to shoot down an - gels.

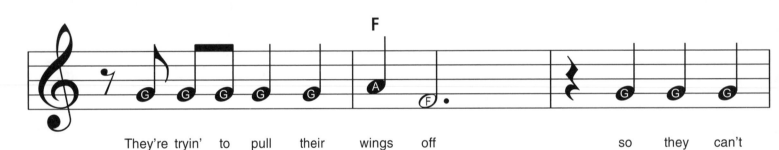

They're tryin' to pull their wings off   so they can't

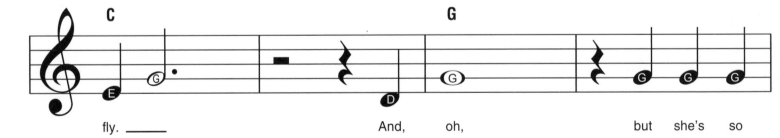

fly. _____   And, oh,   but she's so

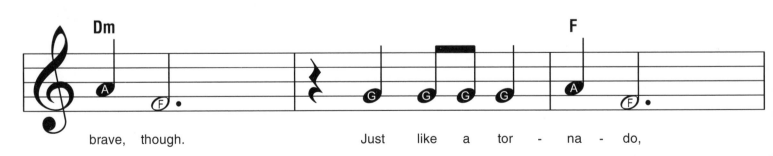

brave, though.   Just like a tor - na - do,

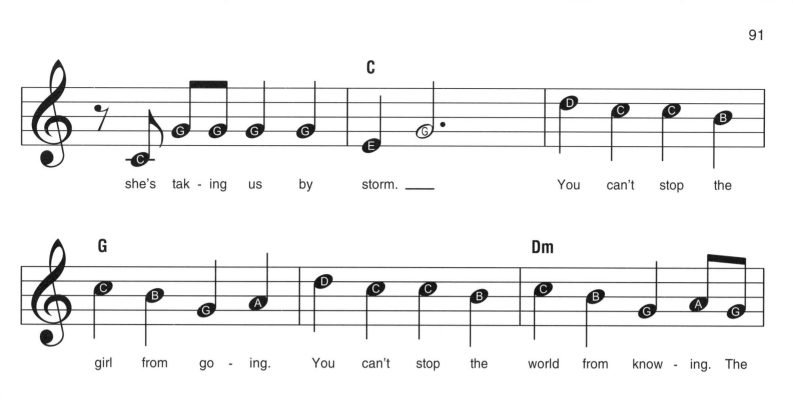

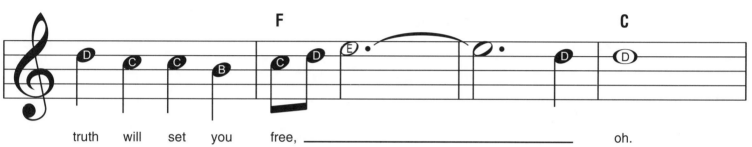

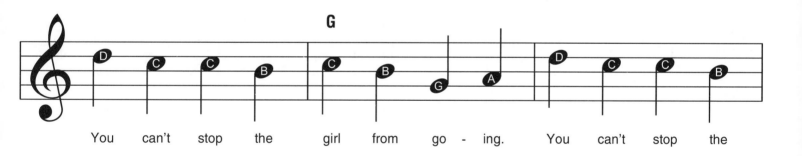

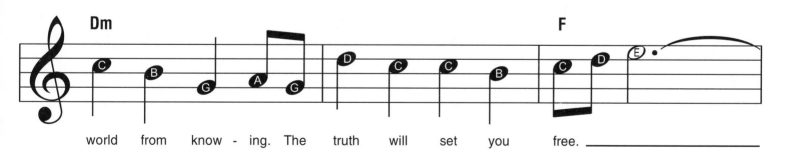

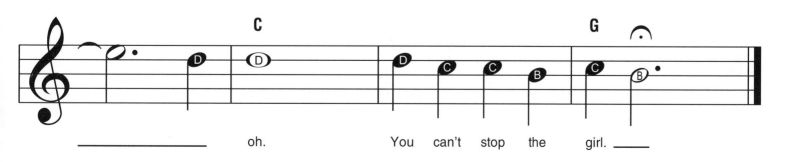

You'll Be in My Heart

(Pop Version)*
from TARZAN

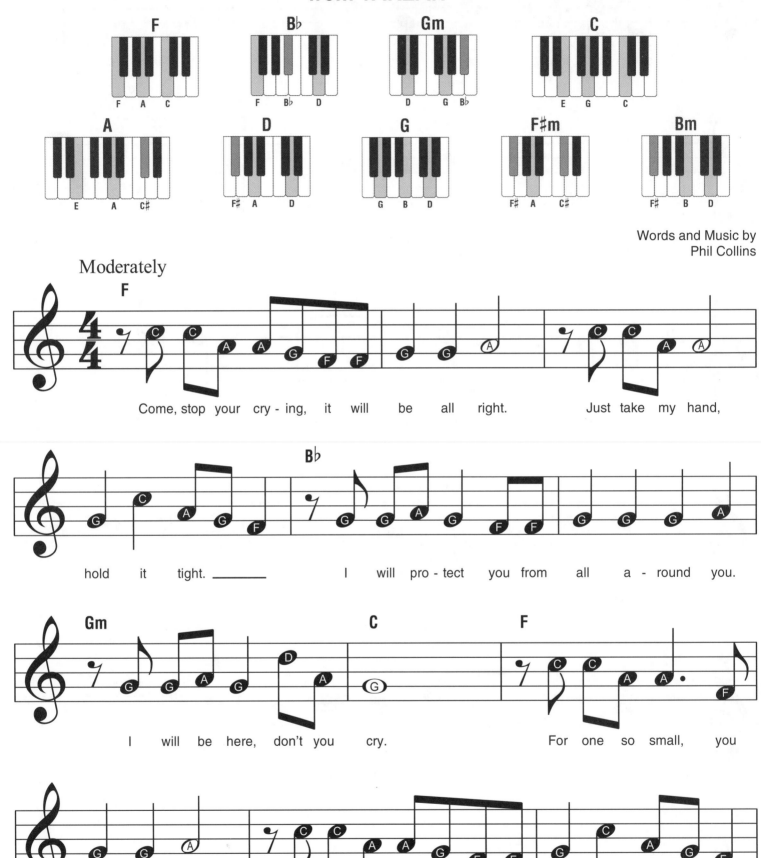

Words and Music by
Phil Collins

Moderately

Come, stop your cry - ing, it will be all right. Just take my hand,

hold it tight. _____ I will pro - tect you from all a - round you.

I will be here, don't you cry. For one so small, you

seem so strong. My arms will hold you, keep you safe and warm. _____

You're Welcome
from MOANA

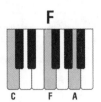
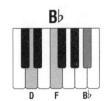
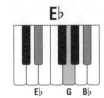

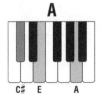

Music and Lyrics by
Lin-Manuel Miranda

Moderate Shuffle

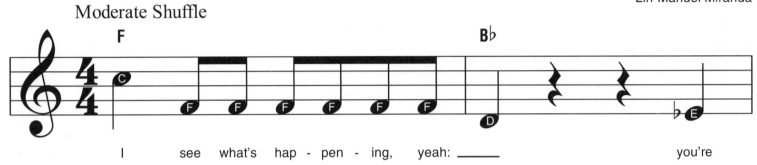

I see what's hap-pen-ing, yeah: _____ you're

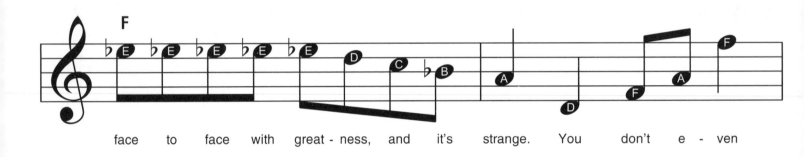

face to face with great-ness, and it's strange. You don't e-ven

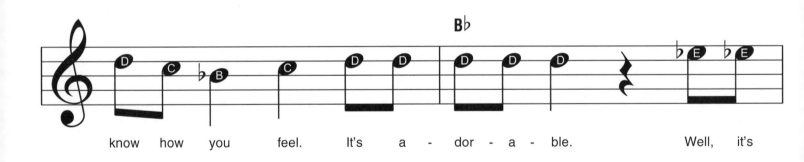

know how you feel. It's a-dor-a-ble. Well, it's

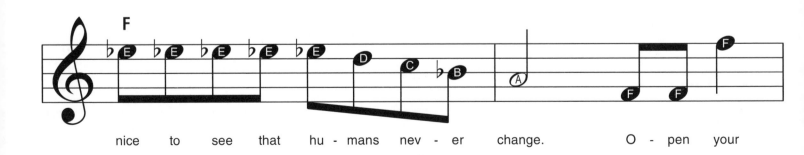

nice to see that hu-mans nev-er change. O-pen your